「我引用旁人的話語，只為了能夠更透徹地表達自己。」

——米歇爾・德・蒙田

引　言

哪些特質能讓一句話夠資格稱作「最有智慧」？也許我們應該問的是：如何定義「智慧」？心思機敏或多謀善斷也許是其中一個定義；但你會發現本書中所列出的每一句話都具有以下的特質：那就是能夠洞悉隱藏在各種表徵之下的人性狀態。

「智慧」也意味著風格獨具（例如我們常說的「妳穿這件洋裝是個有智慧的選擇」，此處的「智慧」有著「很有型」的意思），而本書所選的許多金句在用字上都可說是典雅雋永。智慧也代表著「機智」，它不只是妙趣橫生，更具有著十八世紀理性主義的特質。所以真正的機智，就像當時著名詩人波普（Alexander Pope）所說的，乃是有如「巧手雕琢璞玉，妙語道盡人事」的能耐。而「聰明」也有著「一針見血」的意涵。本書中的許多好句子正是要狠狠地打中讀者的痛處；以一記當頭棒喝讓你看清自己的偏差與成見。

本書將最後一個章節給了諺語，這也許看起來是有些了無新意。但是就本質上來說，諺語本來就與獨創性無關；其所體現的乃是亙久不變的真理。將諺語視為毫無創見或者老生常談，可說是搞錯了重點。諺語經過無數次的引用，也經歷了歲月的洗禮。如果不是蘊含著可以不斷啟發後世的精煉智慧，它們就早已消逝在民間了。

本書所選的名言佳句無論是在書寫上或口語上都被廣泛地引用，因為它們皆觸及了各種層面的人情世故。在〈生與死：以及期間發生的種種〉這一章節中的話語關照了人從降生到死亡的各個過程。〈心靈生命〉這一章則探究了人類的知識運作。而人與人之間的關係則是〈愛與友情〉這章的主題。在〈成功之道〉與〈為政之道：政客抑或政治家？〉這兩個章節中，人類世俗與心靈的層面都受到關照。最後一章〈諺語的智慧〉則是名副其實的俗諺精華，但讀者也會發現其他諺語也出現在相關的章節中。

本書佳句的來源甚廣。也許將莎士比亞（William Shakespeare）、尤吉・貝拉（Yogi Berra，前大聯盟明星棒球員）、聖經、史達林（Joseph Stalin）、艾森豪（Dwight Eisenhower）、基思・理查茲（Keith Richards，英國歌手）和米克・傑格（Mick Jagger，

英國歌手）這些名字湊在一塊看起來有些怪異，但是這僅僅意味著，智慧並非由同一種人所壟斷的。

如何能被本書揀選為最有智慧的一千零一句話之一？本書的準則簡單來說就在於深度和廣度。也許有些讀者對於哪些句子被選入本書中，而哪些沒能入選會有點意見，他們當然有權利表達這樣的意見。而也許有些讀者會更進一步指出，有些句子與其他句子所表達的意思是互相抵觸的（比如說，「別久情更深」與「離久情漸疏」）。然而，矛盾與衝突，原本就是人類智慧的本質之一。

另一個常見的問題則是，在本書中諸多名句中，哪一句話能夠稱得上是第一名？雖然我們很難把智慧想像成某種運動競賽，但是我願意用一部古早的五零年代影集片段來回應這個問題。在《四星劇院》（*Four Star Playhouse*）的某集中，場景設在一間酒吧，一群人在這裡互相慰藉，以一起迎接世界末日（我已經記不得為什麼了，反正那集就是個末世的設定）。其中一個人拿出了一台電腦（這在五零年代可是相當時髦的設備呢！），他在電腦裡儲存了所有的世界文學名著。然後，在其他人的簇擁之下，他對電腦輸入了以下的問題：「我們該如何拯救這個世界？」這台電腦嘰哩咕嚕、燈光閃爍了一陣子（五零年代的玩意兒嘛），然後顯示了答案：「我是耶和華你的神；除了我之外你不可有別的神⋯」接著將摩西十誡一股腦兒地秀出來。這是聖經的一家之言，但在這個情境之中也是發人深省。

五十年的歲月改變了許多事情。但是真正的智慧卻是亙久不變。真理無論在什麼時代都是人們處事的圭臬。在現今這個許多知識都被過度簡化、甚至到反智地步的社會，研讀經過歲月洗禮的智慧，可說是重新建立知識與道德標竿的重要一步。

史蒂芬 D. 普萊斯
2004 年五月 於美國紐約

Contents

第一章
生與死：以及期間發生的種種

CHAPTER I

Life and Death

(...And Some of What Happens in Between)

001

要理解生活，必得回顧過去；但若要活得精彩，
就需著眼未來。

—— 索倫・齊克果（丹麥哲學家，1813-1855）

Life can only be understood backwards, but it must be lived forwards.

—Søren Kierkegaard

002

我們無法超越生與死，唯有揮灑品味這其間的
歲月。

—— 喬治・桑塔亞那（美國哲學家、詩人，1863-1952）

There is no cure for birth and death save to enjoy the interval.

—George Santayana

003

未來會在適當的時機揭露面紗；在此之前，還
是專注於當下吧！

—— 埃斯庫羅斯（希臘悲劇作家，525-456 B. C.）

The future you shall know when it has come; before then forget it.

—Aeschylus

004

一個人的思想構築了他的世界，也決定了他的未來。

—— 古印度《慈氏奧義書》

One's own thought is one's world. What a person thinks is what he becomes. —*Maitri Upanishads*

005

人並非生來睿智；時間使一切事物成長茁壯。

—— 塞萬提斯（西班牙作家，1547-1616）

Time ripens all things; no man is born wise.

—Miguel de Cervantes

006

每一個新生的胎兒都是上帝希望生命永續的明證。

—— 卡爾·桑德堡（美國作家、詩人，1878-1967）

A baby is God's opinion that life should go on. —Carl Sandburg

007

對一個男人來說，生下孩子是件很輕易的事，
但是如何當個真正的好父親才是一大挑戰。

—— 教宗若望二十三世（1881-1963）

It is easier for a father to have children than for children to have a father.
—Pope John XXIII

008

在這世界上我們最需要正視的問題是：「為什
麼有些人一降生就處於淚水與苦難中？」

—— 愛麗絲‧華克（美國小說家，1944-）

The most important question in the world is, "Why is the child crying?"
—Alice Walker

009

作為父母，如果你能夠給予孩子一樣天賦，那
非「熱情」莫屬。

—— 布魯斯‧巴頓（美國議員，1886-1967）

If you can give your son or daughter only one gift, let it be enthusiasm.
—Bruce Barton

010

當你企圖逼迫孩子改變他們的某些特質時，應該想想，也許該檢討或改變的其實是自己。

——卡爾·榮格（瑞士心理學家，1875-1961）

If there is anything we wish to change in the child, we should first examine it and see whether it is not something that could better be changed in ourselves.

—Carl Jung

011

人不能免於被生於平庸，但是不能甘於平庸。

——薩奇·佩吉（美國大聯盟棒球選手，1906-1982）

Ain't no man can avoid being born average, but there ain't no man got to be common.

—Satchel Paige

012

在我們告訴自己的孩子「誠實為上」之前，恐怕得先設法給他們一個誠實的社會。

——華爾特·貝頌爵士
（英國小說家、人道主義者，1836-1901）

I am afraid we must make the world honest before we can honestly say to our children that honesty is the best policy. —Sir Walter Besant

013

從孩子身上我們可以學到很多。比如說，我們耐心的極限究竟在哪。

—— 法蘭克林・亞當斯（美國專欄作家，1881－1960）

You can learn many things from children. How much patience you have, for instance.

—Franklin P. Adams

014

表現出孩童的純真對我們來說是再自然不過了，但是無論我們的年紀增長多少，我們依舊很難表現出所謂「成年人」的一面。

—— 莉莉・湯琳（美國喜劇演員，1936－）

Acting childish seems to come naturally, but acting like an adult, no matter how old we are, just doesn't come easy to us.

—Lily Tomlin

015

只有不斷地成長，才是人生的明證。

—— 約翰・亨利・紐曼（英國神學家，1801－1890）

Growth is the only evidence of life.

—John Henry Newman

016

每一次過生日都是改頭換面的好時機：像丟掉
舊衣服一般，永遠棄絕自己的陳舊陋習吧！

——阿莫士·布朗森·奧爾柯特

（美國教育家、社會改革家，1799－1888）

A birthday is a good time to begin anew: throwing away the old habits,
as you would old clothes, and never putting them on again.

—Bronson Alcott

017

我父親時常說，小孩子需要有四樣東西：愛、
營養的飲食、規律的睡眠和舒服的熱水澡。除
此之外，他們最需要的，就是適度地脫離父母
的束縛。

——艾薇·貝克·普瑞斯特

（前美國財政部財務長，1905－1975）

My father always said there are four things a child needs: plenty of love,
nourishing food, regular sleep, and lots of soap and water.
After that, what he needs most is some intelligent neglect.

—Ivy Baker Priest

018

每個人的生命之中都有許多條道路，而我們最難掌握的，就是該選擇或遠離哪些道路。

—— 大衛·羅素（蘇格蘭古典吉他音樂家，1953–）

The hardest thing to learn in life is which bridge to cross and which to burn.　　　　　　　　　　　　　　　　　　—David Rusell

019

溫暖的人，就如同燦陽般照耀著我們的方寸之地。

—— 華特·惠特曼（美國詩人，1819–1892）

Some people are so much sunshine to the square inch.

—Walt Whitman

020

這世上最難熬的事，莫過於你必須默默地看著某人把事情搞砸。

—— 白修德（美國政治記者、歷史學家，1915–1985）

The most difficult thing in the world is to know how to do a thing and to watch someone else do it wrong, without comment.

—T. H. White

021

如果每個人都專注於自己份內的工作，這世界
進步的速度就會加快不少。

—— 路易斯·卡羅（英國作家，1832-1898）

"If everybody minded their own business," the Duchess said in a hoarse
growl, "the world would go round a good deal faster than it does."

—Lewis Carroll

022

用心經營人生，讓它為你的靈魂在人世間銘刻
下永恆的記憶。

—— 艾伊·蘭德（俄裔美國小說家、哲學家，1905-1982）

Live a life as a monument to your soul.　　　　—Ayn Rand

023

如果你在牌桌上看不出來哪個傢伙是待宰的肥
羊，別懷疑，大家都等著扒你一層皮。

—— 佚名

If you're in a card game and you don't know who the sucker is, you're it.

—Anonymous

024

人生除死無大事，但太多人都沒有膽量在活著
的時候冒險、掌握機會。比起死亡，他們更恐
懼生命本身。

—— 詹姆斯‧F‧伯恩斯（前美國國務卿，1879-1972）

Too many people are thinking of security instead of opportunity.
They seem more afraid of life than death. —James F. Byrnes

025

人與人之間互相幫助，就好像是我們寓居在這
世上該付出的房租。

—— 穆罕默德‧阿里（美國拳擊手，1942-2016）

Service to others is the rent you pay for your room here on earth.
—Muhammad Ali

026

在僕人面前，沒有人能稱得上是英雄。

—— 佚名

No man is a hero to his own valet. —Anonymous

027

只有在人類能夠多欣賞與尊重大自然的美麗與靜謐，而不是花費心力征服她的時候，我才能對未來有更光明的想像。

——E·B·懷特（美國作家，1899－1985）

I would feel more optimistic about a bright future for man if he spent less time proving that he can outwit Nature and more time tasting her sweetness and respecting her seniority.　　——E. B. White

028

真理就像路上一顆毫不起眼的石頭，人們有時會不經意地被它絆倒。然而大多數的人都會迅速起身，裝作什麼事都沒發生。

——溫斯頓·邱吉爾（前英國首相，1874－1965）

Men occasionally stumble over the truth, but most of them pick themselves up and hurry on as if nothing had happened.　　——Sir Winston Churchill

029

每個人在情感上的沸點都不盡相同。

——拉爾夫·沃爾多·愛默生
（美國哲學家、詩人，1803－1882）

We boil at different degrees.　　　　——Ralph Waldo Emerson

030

體認在我們週遭與心中的無形力量，並維持生命的平衡。如果能以此為生活的準則，就能成為真正的智者。

—— 歐里庇得斯（希臘劇作家，480–406 B.C.）

The best and safest thing is to keep a balance in your life, acknowledge the great powers around us and in us. If you can do that, and live that way, you are really a wise man. ——Euripides

031

人生就像一張巨幅的畫布，盡其所能地揮灑各種色彩吧！

—— 丹尼·凱伊（美國喜劇演員、歌手，1911–1987）

Life is a great big canvas; throw all the paint you can at it.

——Danny Kaye

032

從直接面對恐懼的經驗之中，我們得到力量、勇氣與信心。我們能這樣告訴自己：「我已克服過這樣的恐怖經歷，再也沒有任何事能讓我退縮」。

——愛蓮娜·羅斯福
（前美國第一夫人、外交官，1884－1962）

You gain strength, courage and confidence by every experience in which you really stop to look fear in the face. You are able to say to yourself, "I lived through this horror. I can take the next thing that comes along."
　　　　　　　　　　　　　　　　　　—Eleanor Roosevelt

033

音樂之美在於每一個演奏和聆聽的瞬間。而人生也是如此；如果我們太過汲汲營營，將會忘記如何體認到生命之美。

——亞倫·W·華特（美國哲學家，1915－1973）

The point of music is discovered in every moment of playing and listening to it. It is the same, I feel, with the greater part of our lives, and if we are unduly absorbed in improving them we may forget altogether to live them.
　　　　　　　　　　　　　　　　　　—Alan B. Watts

034

幾乎所有人都有能耐克服逆境。但唯有一個人
在順境中掌權的時候,我們才能真正看清他的
品格。

—— 亞伯拉罕・林肯（美國第十六任總統，1809–1865）

Nearly all men can stand adversity, but if you want to test a man's
character, give him power. —Abraham Lincoln

035

大體來說,人性是向善的。但並非時時刻刻都
如此。

—— 喬治・歐威爾（英國小說家、散文家，1903–1950）

On the whole, human beings want to be good, but not too good and
not quite all the time. —George Orwell

036

教育是人在邁向年老時的最大財富。

—— 亞里斯多德（希臘哲學家，384–322 B. C. ）

Education is the best provision for the journey to old age.
—Aristotle

037

從痛苦中成長茁壯是多麼崇高的一件事。
—— 亨利・沃茲沃思・朗費羅（美國詩人，1807–1882）

Know how sublime a thing is to suffer and be strong.
—Henry Wadsworth Longfellow

038

人該在意的不是名聲，而是自己的品格。因為品格代表的是真實的自我，名聲則不過是旁人構築的虛假印象。
—— 約翰・R・伍登（美國大學籃球教練，1910–2010）

Be more concerned with your character than your reputation, because your character is what you really are, while your reputation is merely what others think you are.
—John R. Wooden

039

最為重要的是：對自己誠實，就不會對他人虛偽；正如同白晝與黑夜相輔相成。
—— 威廉・莎士比亞（英國劇作家，1564–1616）

This above all: to thine own self be true,
And it must follow, as the night the day,
Thou canst not then be false to any man.
—William Shakespeare

040

對於知識所能掌握到的事物，我從未感到畏懼。

—— 安娜·席維爾（英國作家，1820－1878）

I am never afraid of what I know. —Anna Sewell

041

莫以驕傲面對謙虛者；莫以謙虛面對驕傲者。

—— 傑佛遜·戴維斯（美國政治家，1808－1889）

Never be haughty to the humble; never be humble to the haughty.

—Jefferson Davis

042

即令是一般人，有時也能夠有超凡的表現。而這就是人類的超凡之處。

—— 喬治·F·威爾（美國政治記者，1941－）

It is extraordinary how extraordinary the ordinary person is.

—George F. Will

043

人類的文明主要是由一連串的契機與創意所構築而成。

——拉爾夫‧沃爾多‧愛默生
（美國哲學家、詩人，1803－1882）

The majority of men are bundles of beginnings.

——Ralph Waldo Emerson

044

思索你的能力、缺失和人際關係，你就能了解人生中當盡的責任，並且引領自己走上正確的道路。

——阿肯那頓
（古埃及第十八王朝法老，－1354 B. C.）

Contemplate thy powers, contemplate thy wants and thy connections, so shalt thou discover the duties of life, and be directed in all thy ways.

——Akhenaton

045

看人看年少；看天看破曉。

——約翰‧米爾頓（英國詩人，1608－1674）

The childhood shows a man, as morning shows the day.

——John Milton

046

年輕人都會面對一個同樣的問題：如何能循規蹈矩，但是同時又表現得瀟灑叛逆？於是，他們一方面模仿父母、一方面又反抗父母。

—— 昆丁·克里斯普（美國自傳作家，1908-1999）

The young always have the same problem—how to rebel and conform at the same time. They have solved this by defying their parents and copying one another. —Quentin Crisp

047

萬物不興則衰、不進則退。

—— 希列爾
（古代希伯來哲學家、神學家，110-10 B.C.）

Who does not grow, declines.

—Rabbi Hillel

048

一個人沒有理由到他四十八歲時，還鍾愛十八歲時讀的書。

—— 艾佐拉·龐德（美國詩人，1885-1972）

There is no reason why the same man should like the same book at 18 and 48. —Ezra Pound

049

如果一個五十歲的人，仍以他二十歲時的眼光看這個世界，那他可說是虛擲了過去三十年的光陰。

——穆罕默德‧阿里（美國拳擊手，1942-2016）

The man who views the world at 50 the same as he did at 20 has wasted thirty years of his life.
——Muhammad Ali

050

如果將世上所有苦難堆成一堆由所有人均分，大多數人都會願意扛起自己的一份，安然離去。

——蘇格拉底（古希臘哲學家，469-399 B.C.）

If all misfortunes were laid in one common heap whence everyone must take an equal portion, most people would be contented to take their own and depart.
——Socrates

051

大多數人並不想成為聖人。而那些期望（或已經）成聖的人，對於世俗與人生都是興趣缺缺。

——喬治‧歐威爾（英國小說家、散文家，1903-1950）

Many people genuinely do not wish to be saints, and it is possible that some who achieve or aspire to sainthood have never had much temptation to be human beings.
——George Orwell

052

當你審視每一天的意義與價值時，看重的應該
是你撒下的種子，而非收穫的果實。

——羅伯特·路易斯·史蒂文生
（英國小說家，1850－1894）

Don't judge each day by the harvest you reap, but by the seeds you plant.　　　　　　　　　　　　　　——Robert Louis Stevenson

053

如果能以再清閒不過的心情去過一再沒有比這
更沒事的午後，那你算懂得怎樣生活了。

——林語堂（中國文學家，1895－1976）

If you can spend a perfectly useless afternoon in a perfectly useless manner, you have learned how to live.　　　　　　——Lin Yutang

054

心靈的平靜能使人視世俗的毀譽如浮雲。

——巴爾扎克（法國小說家、劇作家，1799－1850）

He has great tranquility of heart who cares neither for the praises nor the fault-finding of men.　　　　　　　　　　　——Honoré de Balzac

055

沒有人能在做出決斷前完美地看清所有的情況。痛悔本來就是人生的一部份，我們必須學習接受它。

—— 亨利·腓特烈·愛彌爾
（瑞士哲學家、詩人，1821－1881）

The man who insists upon seeing with perfect clearness before he decides, never decides. Accept life, and you must accept regret.

—— Henri-Frédéric Amiel

056

飛禽走獸能夠逍遙自得的一大原因，就是在於牠們不用處心積慮地想要贏得同類的青睞。

—— 戴爾·卡內基（美國人際關係學家、作家，1888－1955）

One reason why birds and horses are not unhappy is because they are not trying to impress other birds and horses. —Dale Carnegie

057

接受挑戰，意味著你必須捲起袖子，將自己的身心投入人生的漩渦之中。而拒絕挑戰就輕鬆多了，縱使這意味著逃避人生、趨向死亡。

——尚·阿諾伊（*法國劇作家，1910-1987*）

To say yes, you have to sweat and roll up your sleeves and plunge both hands into life up to the elbows. It's easy to say no, even if it means dying.
　　　　　　　　　　　　　　　　　　　　——Jean Anouilh

058

死物終會隨波逐流，唯有生命能夠逆流而上。

——G·K·卻斯特頓（*英國作家，1874-1936*）

A dead thing can go with the stream, but only a living thing can go against it.
　　　　　　　　　　　　　　　　　　　——G. K. Chesterton

059

當我們年少時總會因為一些我們從未犯過的錯而受到指責，年老時卻會因為一些我們從未擁有的美德受到讚揚。這大概也算是公平的吧！

——凱西·史坦哲爾
（*美國大聯盟棒球選手，1890-1975*）

When you are younger you get blamed for crimes you never committed and when you're older you begin to gain credit for virtues you never possessed. It evens itself out.
　　　　　　　　　　　　　　　　　　　——Casey Stengel

060

生命就像是回音一樣；你付出什麼，就會得到
什麼。

——佚名

Life is an echo. What you sent out—you get back. What you give—you
get.　　　　　　　　　　　　　　　　　　——Anonymous

061

人生就好像拉小提琴，無論學習或演奏，都是
在眾目睽睽之下進行。

——塞繆爾・巴特勒（英國詩人、作家，1612-1680）

Life is like playing a violin in public and learning the instrument as one
goes on.

——Samuel Butler

062

人生就好像牌局：重要的不是如何拿到一手好
牌，而是如何運用已經握在手上的牌。

——喬許・畢林斯（美國散文家，1818-1885）

Life consists not in holding good cards but in playing those you hold
well.

——Josh Billings

063

人生就是一段關於寬恕的旅程。

—— 諾曼・考辛斯（美國作家，1915-1990）

Life is an adventure in forgiveness.　　　　　—Norman Cousins

064

人生的藝術就是從許多不足的假設之中，汲取到完善的結論。

—— 塞繆爾・巴特勒（英國詩人、作家，1612-1680）

Life is the art of drawing sufficient conclusions from insufficient premises.

—Samuel Butler

065

如果你不能改善某個狀況，就一笑置之吧！

—— 艾爾瑪・龐貝克（美國作家，1927-1996）

If you can't make it better, you can laugh at it.　　—Erma Bombeck

066

維持一個人的品格比墮落之後再恢復它要容易
得多。

—— 湯瑪斯・潘恩（英裔美國政治家、思想家，1737–1809）

Characters is much easier kept than recovered.　　　—Thomas Paine

067

作為紳士的第一道考驗就是：他是否能對一個
對自己毫無任何好處的人展現出尊重。

—— 威廉・里昂・菲爾普斯
（美國教育家、文學批評家，1865–1943）

This is the first test of a gentleman: his respect for those who can be of
no possible value to him.　　　—William Lyon Phelps

068

所謂的「未來」正隨著每一天的過去而消逝。

—— 迪安・艾奇遜（美國政治家，1893–1971）

The future comes one day at the time.　　　—Dean Acheson

069

自己好好努力，你就不會需要依賴前人的指引。

—— 伏爾泰（法國哲學家，1694-1778）

Do well and you will have no need for ancestors.

—Voltaire

070

這世上最堅強的，就是那些能夠遺世獨立的人。

—— 亨里克·易卜生（挪威劇作家，1828-1906）

The strongest man in the world is he who stands alone.

—Henrik Ibsen

071

一個成熟的人不會只以絕對的準則考慮事情。
他能夠在情緒受到波動時仍能保持客觀，他也
能夠理解善與惡是並存於所有人事物中的。同
時，他能以謙遜且仁善的態度來看待人生百態。

—— 愛蓮娜·羅斯福

（前美國第一夫人、外交官，1884-1962）

A mature person is one who does not think only in absolutes, who is able
to be objective even when deeply stirred emotionally, who has learned
that there is both good and bad in all people and all things, and who
walks humbly and deals with charitably with the circumstances of life.

—Eleanor Roosevelt

072

衡量一個人的準則就在於他如何能在苦難中堅
忍不拔。

——普魯塔克（希臘哲學家、傳記作家，46-120 A. D.）

The measure of a man is the way he bears up under misfortune.

—Plutarch

073

希望在人心中永恆地悸動；福氣也許不在當下，
卻也永恆地在未來等待著。

——亞歷山大·波普
（英國詩人、諷刺文學家，1688-1744）

Hope springs eternal in the human breast: Man never is, but always to be blest.

—Alexander Pope

074

十賭九輸：這就是人生的通則。

——達蒙·魯尼恩（美國記者、作家，1880-1946）

All life is 6 to 5 against.

—Damon Runyon

075

當我們因為顧慮他人的看法而選擇隱瞞真相，
或因為政治因素而不敢仗義執言時，我們的靈
魂就不再受到神的眷顧了。

—— 伊麗莎白·卡迪·斯坦頓
（美國社會改革家、婦女參政運動者，1815-1902）

The moment we begin to fear the opinions of others and hesitate to tell
the truth that is in us, and from motives of policy are silent when we
should speak, the divine floods of light and life no longer flow into our
souls. —Elizabeth Cady Stanton

076

人不僅要為自己做過的事負責，也必須為未做
的事負責。

—— 莫里哀（法國劇作家，1622-1673）

It is not only for what we do that we are held responsible, but also for
what we do not do. —Molière

077

時間就是你最睿智的謀臣。

—— 伯里克里斯
（古希臘雅典政治家，495-429 B.C.）

Time is the wisest counselor. —Pericles

078

人們時常千里跋涉，只為了讚嘆那壯闊的山脈、
洶湧的巨浪、千里綿延的大河、無垠的汪洋、
或者繁星的軌跡。但卻遺忘了人類本身令人驚
嘆之處。

—— 聖奧古斯丁（早期基督教神學家、主教，354–430 A. D.）

People travel to wonder at the height of the mountains, at the huge
waves of the seas, at the long course of the rivers, at the vast compass
of the ocean, at the circular motion of the stars, and yet they pass by
themselves without wondering.

—Saint Augustine

079

隨著年歲增長，我漸漸地不再相信「年紀會帶
來智慧」這句話。

—— H·L·孟肯（美國編輯、評論家，1880–1956）

The older I grow the more I distrust the familiar doctrine that age brings
wisdom.

—H. L. Mencken

080

歡欣吧！人們！歡欣吧！
若你能掌握今日、
內心充實，就能夠昂然說：
明日啊！放馬過來吧！因我已活過今日。
美麗也好、醜惡也罷；無論雨或晴，
我所擁有的喜樂已超越命運。
即令是上天也對過去無能為力；
木已成舟，重要的是我掌握了自己的時刻。

—— 賀拉斯（羅馬詩人，65-8 B. C.）

Happy the man, and happy he alone,
He who can call today his own:
He who, secure within, can say,
Tomorrow do thy worst, for I have lived today.
Be fair or foul or rain or shine
The joys I have possessed, in spite of fate, are mine.
Not Heaven itself upon the past has power,
But what has been, has been, and I have had my hour.

—Horace

081

充滿自信地朝你的夢想前進吧！活出自己想像中的生活。返璞歸真地生活，就能明瞭大自然的規律也是同樣地簡單。

—— 亨利·大衛·梭羅
（美國作家、自然主義者，1817-1862）

Go confidently in the direction of your dreams! Live the life you've imagined. As you simplify your life, the laws of the universe will be simpler.
　　　　　　　　　　　　　　　　—Henry David Thoreau

082

純粹的苦難並不能夠教化人心。如果真是如此，那這將是一個充滿智慧的世界，因為在世上人人皆受苦。面對苦難，我們必須學習的是如何哀悼與理解、學習堅忍、博愛與寬容，以及對於人類脆弱一面的認知。

—— 約瑟夫·艾迪生
（英國散文家、詩人、政治家，1672-1719）

I do not believe that sheer suffering teaches. If suffering alone taught, all the world would be wise, since everyone suffers. To suffering must be added mourning, understanding, patience, love, openness and the willingness to remain vulnerable.
　　　　　　　　　　　　　　　　—Joseph Addison

083

在我能夠面對他人之前，我必須先學會面對自己。這世上唯一不受到多數決制約的，就是自己的良心。

——哈波‧李（美國小說家，1926-2016）

. . . before I can live with other folks I've got to live with myself. The one thing that doesn't abide by majority rule is a person's conscience.

——Harper Lee

084

自傷自憐是最具毀滅性的情緒。再也沒有比深陷於自我的牢籠中更糟糕的事了。

——米莉森‧芬威克（美國外交官、國會議員，1910-1992）

Never feel self-pity, the most destructive emotion there is. How awful to be caught up in the terrible squirrel cage of self.

——Millicent Fenwick

085

正所謂福禍相倚：天使頭上的光圈只要再往下移個幾吋，就成了死刑的絞索。

——佚名

A halo has to fall only a few inches to be a noose. ——Anonymous

086

如果你為了生命中的落日哭泣，你的眼淚將會模糊了能夠欣賞繁星的雙眼。

—— 泰戈爾（印度詩人，1861-1941）

If you cry because the sun has gone out of your life, your tears will prevent you from seeing the stars. —Rabindranath Tagore

087

疏遠自然，人心將變得如鐵石般冷硬；對於萬物的不敬，終將成為對人類本身的蔑視。

—— 路德‧史丹汀‧貝爾（美國印第安作家、教育家、哲學家、Oglala Lakota 部落族長，1868-1939）

A man's heart away from nature becomes hard; lack of respect for growing, living things soon leads to a lack of respect for humans too. —Luther Standing Bear

088

快樂向來只是人生中的副產品；不過是內分泌
系統所節制的情感狀態之一。人生中的快樂是
可遇而不可求；所以你如果感到不快樂，最好
別再因此煩惱。

—— 羅伯遜·戴維斯（加拿大小說家，1913-1995）

Happiness is always a by-product. It is probably a matter of
temperament, and for anything I know it may be glandular. But it is not
something that can be demanded from life, and if you are not happy you
had better stop worrying about it. —Robertson Davies

089

在生活中體驗你的諸多疑問，也許某天你也會
在生活中找到它們的解答。

—— 萊納·瑪利亞·里爾克（德國詩人，1875-1926）

Live your questions now, and perhaps even without knowing it, you will
live along some distant day into your answers. —Rainer Maria Rilke

090

大多數的人都在悄無聲息的絕望中活著。

—— 亨利・大衛・梭羅
（美國作家、自然主義者，1817-1862）

The mass of men lead lives of quiet desperation.

—Henry David Thoreau

091

在無常之風吹起時，願你能有堅實的堤防……
也願你能永保青春。

—— 巴布・狄倫（美國歌手、作詞家，1941-）

May you have a strong foundation when the winds of changes shift …
and may you be forever young.

—Bob Dylan

092

別走上既定的道路，踏上那尚未開拓的陌生之
地，留下一條以自己為名的道路吧！

—— 拉爾夫・沃爾多・愛默生
（美國哲學家、詩人，1803-1882）

Do not go where the path may lead, go instead where there is no path
and leave a trail.

—Ralph Waldo Emerson

093

真正的成長茁壯需要些許的危險來激發。

—— 蓋兒・許伊（美國編輯、記者，1937-）

Growth demands a temporary surrender of security.　　—Gail Sheehy

094

對世事無常當心懷感激，對他人當心無怨忿；
當無懼於雷鳴，傾心聆聽鳥啼。

—— 優比・布雷克（美國作曲家、鋼琴家，1887-1983）

Be grateful for luck. Pay the thunder no mind—listen to the birds. And
don't hate nobody.　　　　　　　　　　　　　　　　—Eubie Blake

095

多想想自己現有的幸福吧，不要在意過去的不
幸。前者每個人都擁有很多，後者每個人也或
多或少經歷過一些。

—— 查爾斯・狄更斯（英國小說家，1812-1870）

Reflect upon your present blessings, of which every man has plenty; not
on your past misfortunes of which all men have some.

—Charles Dickens

096

莫讓昨日之事侵佔了今日的時光。

　　── 威爾‧羅傑斯（美國喜劇演員，1879-1935）

Never let yesterday use up too much of today.　　　──Will Rogers

097

我能夠抗拒一切，但誘惑除外。

　　── 奧斯卡‧王爾德（愛爾蘭文學家，1854-1900）

I can resist everything except temptation.　　　──Oscar Wilde

098

如果你想要在人生中獲得成功，你只需要兩樣
特質：無知與自信。

　　── 馬克‧吐溫（美國作家，1835-1910）

To succeed in life, you need two things: ignorance and confidence.
　　　　　　　　　　　　　　　　　　　　　──Mark Twain

099

別對人生有任何期待；卑微地依賴意想不到的
驚喜吧。

—— 愛麗絲・華克（美國小說家，1944-）

Expect nothing. Live frugally on surprise.　　　　　—Alice Walker

100

人必須謹慎選擇自已想要面對怎樣的敵人。

—— 奧斯卡・王爾德（愛爾蘭文學家，1854-1900）

A man cannot be too careful in his choice of enemies.

—Oscar Wilde

101

成功的最大秘訣就在於，以永不疲憊的態度面
對人生。

—— 阿爾伯特・史懷哲（德／法國神學家、醫學家、諾貝爾
和平獎得主，1875-1964）

A great secret of success is to go through life as a man who never gets
used up.　　　　　　　　　　　　　　　　　　—Albert Schweitzer

102

相信自我，你就能明瞭該如何生活。

—— 歌德（德國戲劇家、詩人，1749-1832）

Just trust yourself, then you will know how to live.

—Johann Wolfgang von Goethe

103

一個心存善念且對於自己的能力不過度自信的人，如果能夠堅定自己的生活方式，就能夠享有一個深沈、靜謐且豐富的人生。人生之道最重要的就是為自己而活，過去是如此，未來也會如是。

—— 亨利・米勒（美國作家，1891-1980）

A man of good will with a little effort and belief in his own powers can enjoy a deep, tranquil, rich life—provided he go his own way. . . . To live one's own life is still the best way of life, always was, and always will be.

—Henry Miller

104

如果我還有成長的空間，願我能更為堅強、簡樸、沈靜與溫暖。

—— 道格·哈瑪紹

（瑞典外交家、前聯合國秘書長，1905-1961）

If only I may grow: firmer, simpler—quieter, warmer.

—Dag Hammarskjöld

105

你可以逃離追在身後的事物，但是你無法逃離自己內心中的陰影。

—— 盧安達諺語

You can outdistance that which is running after you, but not what is running inside you.　　　　　　—Rwandan proverb

106

三有無常如秋雲，眾生生死等觀戲，眾生壽行如空電，猶崖瀑布疾速行。

—— 釋迦牟尼（佛教創始者，563-483 B. C. ）

This existence of ours is as transient as autumn clouds. To watch the birth and death of beings is like looking at the movements of a dance. A lifetime is a flash of lightning in the sky. Rushing by, like a torrent down a steep mountain.　　　　　　—Buddha

107

我們若能對世事無常一笑置之，並好好生活，
又何懼於死神？

—— 查理・布考斯基
（德裔美國小說家、詩人，1920-1994）

We are here to laugh at the odds and live our lives so well that Death
will tremble to take us.　　　　　　　—Charles Bukowski

108

死亡根本不算什麼。因為當我們還存在時，他
還未降臨；而等他現身時，我們已經不在了。

—— 伊比鳩魯（希臘哲學家，341-270 B.C.）

Death is nothing to us, since when we are, death has not come, and
when death has come, we are not.　　　　　　　—Epicurus

109

我們皆不過是風中殘燭。

—— 日本諺語

We are no more than candles burning in the wind.

—Japanese proverb

110

無愧於心地去生活，所以即令是家中學舌的鸚鵡落入八卦小人的手中，你也凜然無懼。

—— 威爾・羅傑斯（美國喜劇演員，1879-1935）

Live so that you wouldn't be ashamed to sell the family parrot to the town gossip. —Will Rogers

111

人人都想長命百歲，卻無人想面臨衰老。

—— 班傑明・富蘭克林（美國政治家、作家，1706-1790）

All would live long, but none would be old. —Benjamin Franklin

112

一位大師能夠透過自我節制，來真正顯露出技藝。

—— 歌德（德國戲劇家、詩人，1749-1832）

It is in self-limitation that a master first shows himself.
—Johann Wolfgang von Goethe

113

長遠來看，我們在從生到死的旅程中都不斷地形塑自我與人生。我們最終都要為自己的選擇負起責任。

———愛蓮娜·羅斯福
（前美國第一夫人、外交官，1884-1962）

In the long run, we shape our lives, and we shape ourselves. The process never ends until we die. And the choices we make are ultimately our own responsibility.
———Eleanor Roosevelt

114

一同渡過衰老的時光，能夠讓兩位點頭之交成為真正的朋友。

———羅根·皮爾薩爾·史密斯（美國散文家，1865-1946）

The mere process of growing old together will make the slightest acquaintance seem a bosom friend.
———Logan Pearsall Smith

115

成為自己想要成為的人，永遠都不會嫌晚。

———喬治·艾略特（英國小說家，1819-1880）

You are never too old to be what you might have been.
———George Eliot

116

早知道我能夠活這麼多年，當初應該要好好照顧自己的身體。

—— 米奇·曼托（前美國大聯盟棒球員，1931-1995）

If I knew I was going to live this long, I'd have taken better care of myself.
—Mickey Mantle

117

我走入樹林之中，因為我希望從容不迫地生活，僅僅面對生活中最基本的事實，看看自己能否聆聽其教誨。而不是在臨終之前，才發現自己從未真正地生活過。

—— 亨利·大衛·梭羅
（美國作家、自然主義者，1817-1862）

I went to the woods because I wished to live deliberately, to front only the essential facts of life and see if I could not learn what they had to teach; and not, when I came to die, discover that I had not lived.
—Henry David Thoreau

118

人有好有壞，但是到頭來每個人的終局都是一樣的。

—— 佚名

People—some good, some bad, but in the long run we come out even.
　　　　　　　　　　　　　　　　　　　　　　—Anonymous

119

所有有關死亡的所有名言佳句都有一個大問題，那就是他們都是由活著的人所說的。

—— 佚名

The trouble with quotes about death is that 99.999 percent of them are made by people who are still alive.　　　　—Anonymous

120

就像美好的一天帶來好眠，美好的人生也會帶來善終。

—— 李奧納多·達文西
（義大利藝術家、發明家，1492–1519）

As a well-spent day brings happy sleep, so a life well spent brings happy death.　　　　　　　　　　　　　—Leonardo da Vinci

121

在一位藝術家的人生中，死亡也許並非是最需要煩惱的事。

—— 文森·梵谷（荷蘭畫家，1853－1890）

In an artist's life, death is perhaps not the most difficult thing.

—Vincent van Gogh

122

最後的長眠？不，死亡乃是最後的覺醒。

—— 華爾特·司各特爵士（蘇格蘭小說家，1771－1832）

Death—the last sleep? No, it is the final awakening.

—Sir Walter Scott

123

上帝呀！時光究竟是如何流逝的？就像生命一樣，如果我們稍不注意就轉瞬即逝，反之則是度日如年。

—— 約翰·史坦貝克（美國小說家，1902－1968）

Lord, how the day passes! It's like a life—so quickly when we don't watch it and so slowly if we do.

—John Steinbeck

124

不安於室，就是人類邪惡的一大來源。

—— 帕斯卡（法國哲學家，1623-1662）

I have discovered that all human evil comes from this: man's being
unable to sit still and quiet in a room alone.　　　—Blaise Pascal

125

聽說在東方有一位君主，要他睿智的大臣們想
出一句可以適用於所有時代與情境的箴言。他
得到的那句話是：「而此真理也終將消逝」。

—— 亞伯拉罕・林肯（美國第十六任總統，1809-1865）

It is said an Eastern monarch once charged his wise men to invent him
a sentence, to be ever in view, and which should be true and appropriate
in all times and situations. They presented him the words: And this, too,
shall pass away.　　　—Abraham Lincoln

126

沒有人是一座自給自足的孤島；每個人都是一整塊大陸的一部分。如果一幢房屋、一片岬角，甚或一顆石頭被沖入海中，歐洲也不再完整。任何一個人的死亡都削減了我的存在，因為我與全人類同在。所以當遠處喪鐘響起時，無須探聽，因為那就是為你而響的。

——約翰‧多恩（英國玄學派詩人，1572-1631）

No man is an Island, entire of itself; every man is a piece of the Continent, a part of the main; if a clod be washed away by the sea, Europe is the less, as well as if a promontory were, as well as if a manor of thy friends or of thine own were; any man's death diminishes me, because I am involved in Mankind; And therefore never send to know for whom the bell tolls; It tolls for thee.　　　　—John Donne

127

用心生活，才不會充滿悔恨地渡過漫漫長夜。

——D‧H‧勞倫斯（英國小說家，1885-1930）

I want to live my life so that my nights are not full of regrets.
　　　　—D. H. Lawrence

128

我決心要繼續活下去，好像能夠長生不死一般。
消逝的年歲並不會使人真正衰老。放棄自己的
理想才會。年歲也許會使皮膚皺摺，但是放棄
生活的理想會使靈魂乾枯。

—— 道格拉斯·麥克阿瑟（美國將軍，1880-1964）

I promise to keep on living as though I expected to live forever. Nobody grows old by merely living a number of years. People grow old by deserting their ideals. Years may wrinkle the skin, but to give up wrinkles the soul.
　　　　　　　　　　　　　　　　—Douglas MacArthur

129

願你一生中的每一天都是充實地渡過。

—— 強納森·史威夫特（英國作家，1667-1745）

May you live all the days of your life.　　　　—Jonathan Swift

130

簡樸地生活，並想想世上有許多人僅能勉強地
維持生計。

—— 甘地（印度民族主義領袖，1869-1948）

Live simply, that others may simply live.　　　—Mohandas Gandhi

131

堅持所選。

—— 羅伯特・克魯伯（美國漫畫家、音樂家，1943-）

Keep on truckin'. —Robert Crumb

132

「希望」是頓美好的早餐，但是作為晚餐可就讓人食不下嚥了。

—— 法蘭西斯・培根爵士
（英國哲學家、散文作家，1561-1626）

Hope is a good breakfast, but it is a bad supper. —Sir Francis Bacon

133

我給你個建議：別探究原因或者該不該，盡情享受眼前的美好吧。這就是我生活的哲學。

—— 桑頓・懷爾德（美國小說家、劇作家，1897-1975）

My advice to you is not to inquire why or whither, but just enjoy your ice cream while it's on your plate—that's my philosophy.

—ThorntonWilder

134

青春年華勸君享，
煩惱苦痛待天聽。
時光轉瞬道真言：
飛鳥流離昔巢空。

—— 亨利·沃茲沃思·朗費羅（美國詩人，1807-1882）

Enjoy the spring of love and youth,
To some good angel leave the rest;
For time will teach thee soon the truth,
There are no birds in last year's nest.

—Henry Wadsworth Longfellow

135

體會到時間的真正價值：掌握並享受每一個當
下。揚棄閒晃、懶惰與延宕，永遠不要將昨日
的工作拖延到今日。

—— 菲力·史丹何普·切斯特菲伯爵
（英國作家、政治家，1694-1773）

Know the true value of time; snatch, seize, and enjoy every moment
of it. No idleness, no laziness, no procrastination: never put off till tomorrow what you can do to-day.

—Philip Dormer Stanhope, Lord Chesterfield

136

切莫以怨憤看待過去，也不要以恐懼面對未來，
而是以專注與警覺活在當下。

—— 詹姆斯・瑟伯（美國作家、漫畫家，1894-1961）

Let us not look back in anger, nor forward in fear, but around in
awareness. —James Thurber

137

「經驗」是一位嚴厲的教師。在告訴你道理之
前，他會先狠狠地教訓你一頓。

—— 佚名

Experience is a hard teacher. She gives the test first and the lessons
afterwards. —Anonymous

138

一個人有再多的財富也買不回他的過去。

—— 奧斯卡・王爾德（愛爾蘭文學家，1854-1900）

No man is rich enough to buy back his past. —Oscar Wilde

139

在苦難的時節中，想想我們過去已經歷過的難關，也許會是些許的安慰與幫助。

—— 保羅·哈維（美國廣播電台主播，1918－2009）

In times like these, it helps to recall that there have always been times like these.
—Paul Harvey

140

展開旅程吧！奮勇向前……除此之外別無他法。

—— 田納西·威廉斯（美國劇作家，1911－1983）

Make voyages! Attempt them . . . there's nothing else.
—Tennessee Williams

141

人生中最美好的部分就在於那看似渺小、無可名狀，且未曾被記得的愛與善意。

—— 威廉·華滋華斯（英國浪漫主義詩人，1770－1850）

The best portion of a good man's life is his little, nameless, unremembered acts of kindness and of love.
—William Wordsworth

142

五十歲到七十歲之間的歲月是最難熬的。許多繁瑣的事總是找上門來，而你還沒老到可以理所當然地拒絕它們。

——T‧S‧艾略特（英國詩人，1885－1968）

The years between fifty and seventy are the hardest. You are always being asked to do things, and yet you are not decrepit enough to turn them down.

——T. S. Eliot

143

人啊，就像各式各樣的酒，有些慢慢變成陳年舊醋，有些則是越老越香。

—— 教宗若望二十三世（1881－1963）

Men are like wine, some turn to vinegar, but the best improve with age.

——Pope John XXIII

144

執我之手共年月；待嚐未盡人生樂。

—— 羅勃特‧白朗寧（英國詩人，1812－1889）

Grow old along with me!
The best is yet to be.

——Robert Browning

145

對我來說，這世上唯一通情達理的人就是我的裁縫了。每次我們見面他都翻新對我的衡量標準。其餘人則以其既定成見，期待我去配合他們。

—— 蕭伯納（愛爾蘭劇作家、文學批評家，1856-1950）

The only man who behaves sensibly is my tailor; he takes my measure anew every time he sees me, whilst all the rest go on with their old measurements, and expect them to fit me.

—George Bernard Shaw

146

如果你想要活得長久、活得有收穫，秘訣就在於每天睡前寬恕一切曾令你不快的人事物。

—— 伯納德‧巴魯克
（美國金融家、政策顧問，1870-1965）

One of the secrets of a long and fruitful life is to forgive everybody everything every night before you go to bed.

—Bernard Mannes Baruch

147

年老之人也自有其力量與魅力。

—— 貝蒂・戴維斯（美國演員，1908-1989）

Old age ain't no place for sissies.

—Bette Davis

148

千萬別回頭張望，威脅將潛伏而至。

—— 薩奇・佩吉（美國大聯盟棒球選手，1906-1982）

Don't look back. Something might be gaining on you.

—Satchel Paige

149

切莫著急或煩惱。你不過是這世上匆匆的過客，
所以記得要停下腳步，聞聞花香。

—— 華爾特・哈根（美國職業高爾夫選手，1892-1969）

Don't hurry, don't worry. You're here for a short visit. So be sure to stop
and smell the flowers.

—Walter Hagen

150

盡可能地不斷活下去吧！不到最後關頭都不要
放棄生命。

—— 詹姆士·布朗（美國靈魂樂歌手，1933-2006）

Live as long as you can. Die when you can't help it.

—James Brown

151

在最後審判日時，每個人都得交代為何在生前
沒去享受那些律法所允許之事。

——《塔木德》（猶太教文獻）

A person will be called to account on Judgment Day for every
permissible thing he might have enjoyed but did not.

—*The Talmud*

152

有許多人連在一個下雨的週日午後要做什麼事
都毫無頭緒，卻渴望著長生不死。

—— 蘇珊·艾慈（英國小說家，1894-1985）

Millions long for immortality who do not know what to do with
themselves on a rainy Sunday afternoon.

—Susan Ertz

153

老年和其他事物一樣，要使之成功，必須從年輕時開始。

——佛雷‧亞斯坦（美國舞蹈家、演員，1899-1987）

Old age is like everything else. To make a success of it, you've got to start young.
——Fred Astaire

154

既然我們無法超越時間流動的速度，讓我們歡欣鼓舞來向其消逝致敬。

——歌德（德國戲劇家、詩人，1749-1832）

Since time is not a person we can overtake when he is past, let us honor him with mirth and cheerfulness of heart while he is passing.
——Johann Wolfgang von Goethe

155

讓我告訴你一個秘密吧：別等待末日，因為活著的每天都是末日。

——卡繆（法國存在主義哲學家，1913-1960）

I shall tell you a great secret my friend. Do not wait for the last judgement, it takes place every day.
——Albert Camus

156

遊手好閒是通往死亡的捷徑；辛勤努力則是生命之道。前者愚昧；後者睿智。

—— 釋迦牟尼（佛教創始者，563-483 B.C.）

To be idle is a short road to death and to be diligent is a way of life; foolish people are idle, wise people are diligent.

—Buddha

157

我對於活著會一直保持著不可抑制的欲望，直到我能夠確認這世界因我的存在而更為完善。

—— 亞伯拉罕·林肯（美國第十六任總統，1809-1865）

I have in irrepressible desire to live till I can be assured that the world is a little better for my having lived in it.

—Abraham Lincoln

158

人是唯一會臉紅的動物。或者說，我們需要羞恥感的存在。

—— 馬克·吐溫（美國作家，1835-1910）

Man is the only animal that blushes. Or needs to.

—Mark Twain

159

人生的悲劇並不在於我們受到什麼苦，而在於我們錯過了什麼。

—— 湯瑪斯‧卡萊爾（英國歷史學家，1795-1881）

The tragedy of life is not so much what men suffer, but rather what they miss.
—Thomas Carlyle

160

早死是人生最棒的一件事了，但它還是越晚來越好。

—— 蕭伯納（愛爾蘭劇作家、文學批評家，1856-1950）

The greatest thing in life is to die young—but delay it as long as possible.
—George Bernard Shaw

161

我喜歡活著的感覺。有時候我感覺到自己深陷於極度的不幸與悲傷中，但在經歷過這些之後，我還是能堅定地了解到：僅僅是活著，就是一件崇高的事。

—— 阿嘉莎‧克莉絲蒂（英國推理小說家，1890-1976）

I like living. I have sometimes been wildly, despairingly, acutely miserable, racked with sorrow, but through it all I still know quite certainly that just to be alive is a grand thing.
—Agatha Christie

162

如果能盡情享受生命中的喜樂，一個女人就永遠不需要梳妝打扮。

——羅莎琳‧羅素（美國演員，1912-1976）

Taking joy in life is a woman's best cosmetic.　　——Rosalind Russell

163

人生中最痛快的事，莫過於勇於去做旁人認為你做不到的事。

——沃爾特‧白芝浩（英國經濟學家、散文家，1826-1877）

The greatest pleasure in life is doing what people say you cannot do.

——Walter Bagehot

164

人生和電影最大的差別就在於：劇本需要符合常理，而人生卻非如此。

——約瑟夫‧L‧孟威茲
（美國劇作家、導演，1909-1993）

The difference between life and the movies is that a script has to make sense, and life doesn't.

——Joseph L. Mankiewicz

165

千萬別滿足於既定的思考迴路，而是必須要了解到在框架之外有更寬廣的可能性。

—— 珀爾・貝利（美國歌手、演員，1918-1990）

Never, never rest contented with any circle of ideas, but always be certain that a wider one is still possible. —Pearl Bailey

166

我對於那些常常說「死亡不算什麼」的人感到厭煩。死亡是真切的事實。它代表著任何事的發生都會帶來不可逆的結果。那些輕視死亡的人也將無法慎重地衡量生命。

—— C・S・路易斯（英國作家，1898-1963）

It is hard to have patience with people who say There is no death or Death doesn't matter. There is death. And whatever is matters. And whatever happens has consequences, and it and they are irrevocable and irreversible. You might as well say that birth doesn't matter.

—C. S. Lewis

167

要衡量一個人，與其看他如何回答問題，不如看他如何提出問題。

—— 伏爾泰（法國哲學家，1694-1778）

Judge a man by his questions rather than his answers.　　—Voltaire

168

事物的表象通常都與其本質相差甚遠。

—— 威廉・S・吉伯特爵士
（英國劇作家、歌劇作詞家、詩人，1836-1911）

Things are seldom what they seem.　　—Sir William S. Gilbert

169

好的建議通常都是由一個老到無法做壞榜樣的傢伙提出的。

—— 法蘭索瓦・德・拉羅希福可
（法國作家，1613-1680）

Good advice is something a man gives when he is too old to set a bad example.　　—François de La Rochefoucauld

170

未道之言與未竟之事，乃是人在墳墓前灑下的
最苦澀的淚水。

——哈里特·比徹·斯托
（美國作家、廢奴主義者，1811-1896）

The bitterest tears shed over graves are for words left unsaid and deeds
left undone.　　　　　　　　　　　　　　——Harriet Beecher Stowe

171

上帝不只玩骰子，他還把骰子扔在人們看不到
的角落。

——史蒂芬·霍金（英國理論物理學家、宇宙學家，1942-）

God not only plays dice, he throws them in the corner where you can't
see them.　　　　　　　　　　　　　　　　——Stephen Hawking

172

就道德來說，唯一存在的法則就是：你的行為
必須要發自內心的意志與理性，並且符合普世
的法則與價值。

——康德（德國哲學家，1724-1804）

There is, therefore, only one categorical imperative. It is: Act only
according to that maxim by which you can at the same time will that it
should become a universal law.　　　　　　　　——Immanuel Kant

173

如果每一個人都能毫不猶豫地投入改善世界的
行列，這將是多麼地美好。

—— 安妮·法蘭克
（德國二次大戰時期日記作家，1929-1945）

How wonderful it is that nobody need wait a single moment before
starting to improve the world.　　　　　　　　　—Anne Frank

174

君子求諸己，小人求諸人。

—— 孔子（中國哲學家，551-479 B.C.）

What the superior man seeks is in himself. What the mean man seeks is
in others.　　　　　　　　　　　　　　　　　—Confucius

175

勇氣具有十足的感染力。當一位勇者挺身而出
時，其他人也會感到有為者亦若是。

—— 葛培理（美國福音教派牧師，1918-）

Courage is contagious. When a brave man takes a stand, the spines of
others are stiffened.　　　　　　　　　　　　—Billy Graham

176

自欺要比欺人更接近人類的本性。

—— 杜斯妥也夫斯基（俄國小說家，1821-1881）

Lying to ourselves is more deeply ingrained than lying to others.
—Fyodor Mikhaylovich Dostoyevsky

177

懦夫在真正死亡之前，就已死過多次了；而勇者一生只會嚐過一次死亡的滋味。

—— 威廉·莎士比亞（英國劇作家，1564-1616）

Cowards die many times before their deaths; The valiant never taste death but once.　　　　　　　　　—William Shakespeare

178

像地獄之門般叫人厭惡的，就是那些口是心非的傢伙。

—— 荷馬（古希臘詩人，約西元前八世紀-九世紀）

Hateful to me as the gates of Hades is that man who hides one thing in his heart and speaks another.　　　　　　—Homer

179

唯有當你直視自己內心時，你的雙眼才會明亮。
只看見外在的人，猶如在夢中；而能夠審視內
心的人，才是覺醒地生活著。

—— 榮格（瑞士心理學家，1875-1961）

Your vision will become clear only when you can look into your own
heart. Who looks outside, dreams; who looks inside, awakens.

—Carl Jung

180

睿智地思考，但卻愚莽地行動，此乃人之天性。

—— 安那托爾‧佛朗士（法國詩人、小說家，1844-1924）

It is a human nature to think wisely and act foolishly.

—Antatole France

181

凡事都應該以單純的方式表達，但事物本身絕
非簡單。

—— 愛因斯坦（猶太裔美國物理學家，1879-1955）

Everything should be as simple as it is, but not simpler.

—Albert Einstein

182

人必須要能夠獨立生活，但也需要好的同伴。

—— 查爾斯‧埃文斯‧休斯（美國政治家，1862-1948）

A man has to live with himself, and he should see to it that he always
has good company.　　　　　　　　　　　　—Charles Evans Hughes

183

累積財富與生兒育女能夠點妝現世，但是持續
施行好的事功，才是在真主眼中值得報償與希
望的善舉。

—《古蘭經》

Wealth and children are the adornment of this present life, but good
works, which are lasting, are better in the sight of thy Lord as to
recompense, and better as to hope.　　　　　　　　　　—*The Koran*

184

如果你知道如何享受人生，將會發現生活中處
處是驚喜與讚嘆。

—— 雷‧布萊伯利（美國科幻小說家，1920-2012）

If you enjoy living, it is not difficult to keep the sense of wonder.

—Ray Bradbury

185

文字能促進思考；音樂能激發情感。所以一首好歌能使聽者以感性的方式思考。

——E・Y・哈伯格（美國流行樂作詞家，1896－1981）

Words make you think a thought. Music makes you feel a feeling. A song makes you feel a thought.　　　　　　　　—E.Y. Harburg

186

憂慮就好像一張搖椅：它讓你晃來晃去，卻始終只是原地踏步。

——佚名

Worry is like a rocking chair, it will give you something to do, but it won't get you anywhere.　　　　　　　　—Anonymous

187

沈默也是爭辯的一種方式。

——恩內斯托・切・格瓦拉（古巴革命領袖，1928－1967）

Silence is argument carried on by other means.

—Ernesto "Che" Guevara

188

刻意唱反調，也可說是一種形式的模仿。

—— 喬治・克里斯多夫・李奇坦伯格
（德國物理學家、諷刺作家，1742－1799）

To do just the opposite is also a form of imitation.

—Georg Christoph Lichtenberg

189

溫文的舉止顯現紳士的心性。透過觀察一個人的行為，我們能對他的品格一覽無遺。

—— 愛德蒙・史賓賽（英國詩人，1552－1599）

The gentle mind by gentle deeds is known. For a man by nothing is so well betrayed, as by his manners. —Edmund Spenser

190

在你被某人激怒時，你在無形中也受制於他了。

—— 伊麗莎白・肯尼（美國護理師、作家，1886－1952）

He who angers you conquers you. —Elizabeth Kenny

191

依照自己的本心與理性去堅持一個信念，而非
盲目依循一些古老的典籍、國家的信仰，或幼
時被灌輸的成見。在你理解透徹此信念，並能
以此為善之後，堅定地去貫徹實行，並使更多
的人跟隨你。

——釋迦牟尼（佛教創始者，563－483 B. C.）

Believe not because some old manuscripts are produced, believe not
because it is your national belief, believe not because you have been
made to believe from your childhood, but reason truth out, and after you
have analyzed it, then if you find it will do good to one and all, believe
it, live up to it and help others live up to it.　　　　　——Buddha

192

善惡之間的分際，在每個人的心中刻下一道鴻
溝。人要去惡行善，須得粉碎自己內心險惡的
一部份，而這有幾人能夠做到？

—— 亞歷山大·索忍尼辛（俄國作家，1918－2008）

The line dividing good and evil cuts through the heart of every human
being. And who is willing to destroy a piece of his own heart?

——Aleksandr Solzhenitsyn

193

恕者，及與敵為和者，真主必賞之；蓋行不義者不得天寵者也。

——《古蘭經》

He who forgiveth, and is reconciled unto his enemy, shall receive his reward from God; for he loveth not the unjust doers.

——*The Koran*

194

人心之初就好似白紙一般，沒有任何性格與想法。而如何為這張白紙增添色彩？我的答案是：經驗。

—— 約翰·洛克（英國實證主義哲學家，1632–1704）

Let us then suppose the mind to be, as we say, a white paper, void of all characters, without any ideas. How comes it to be furnished? . . . To this I answer, in one word, from experience. ——John Locke

195

擾害己家的，必承受清風；愚昧人必作慧心人的僕人。

——《聖經》（箴言第十一章第二十九節，中文和合本）

He that troubleth his own house shall inherit the wind.

——*The Bible*, Proverbs 11:29

196

每個人都能克服悲傷，除了身在其中之人。

——威廉‧莎士比亞（英國劇作家，1564－1616）

Everyone can master a grief but he that has it.　—William Shakespeare

197

當我漫步走過這世界，
我遇到好些有趣的傢伙：
有些人持槍威脅你交出錢財，
有些人則是用一支鋼筆，
就讓你傾家盪產。＊

——伍迪‧葛瑟瑞（美國創作歌手，1912－1967）

As through this world I rambled
I've seen lots of funny men.
Some will rob you with a six-gun
And some with a fountain pen.

　　　　　　　　　　　　　—Woody Guthrie

＊ 出自葛瑟瑞的歌曲「The Ballad of Pretty Boy Floyd」。歌
　曲中將美國大蕭條時期的著名罪犯佛洛伊德（Charles Arthur
　Floyd）浪漫化為劫富濟貧的英雄，並諷刺資產階級對勞工的
　敲詐與剝削比強盜要更為邪惡。

198

臉上的一陣潮紅也許會讓一個娼妓被錯認為良家婦女；謙遜則是會讓一個愚者看起來像是個有條理的人。

—— 強納森·史威夫特（英國諷刺作家，1667-1745）

As blushing will sometimes make a whore pass for a virtuous woman, so modesty may make a fool seem a man of sense.　　　—Jonathan Swift

199

人生如果少了音樂，就好像在荒漠中獨行一般。

—— 帕特·康羅伊（美國作家，1945-2016）

Without music, life is a journey through a desert.　　　—Pat Conroy

200

我們漸漸會發現，人生中真正重要的時刻，並非是那些引人注目的日子——生日、畢業典禮或婚禮——也非那些你取得偉大成就的時刻。人生中真正的里程碑其實低調的很。它們輕敲那未被注意的記憶之門：好似一些流浪狗悄悄溜進來，四處嗅嗅然後安然住下。我們的人生就是由這些不經意的時刻所悄然建構。

——蘇珊·B·安東尼（美國婦女參政運動者，1820–1906）

Sooner or later we all discover that the important moments in life are not the advertised ones, not the birthdays, the graduations, the weddings, not the great goals achieved. The real milestones are less prepossessing. They come to the door of memory unannounced, stray dogs that amble in, sniff around a bit and simply never leave. Our lives are measured by these.

　　　　　　　　　　　　　　　　　　　　　—Susan B. Anthony

201

盡可能地在健康的時候揮灑生命，甚至筋疲力盡也在所不惜。因為這就是生命的意義。在死亡前散盡一切所有吧！別在一具空殼中苟活。

——蕭伯納（愛爾蘭劇作家、文學批評家，1856–1950）

Use your health, even to the point of wearing it out. That is what it is for. Spend all you have before you die; and do not outlive yourself.

　　　　　　　　　　　　　　　　　　　—George Bernard Shaw

202

殺害一個生命的罪孽就好像毀滅整個世界一樣
深重。而拯救一個生命的義舉就好像挽救整個
世界一樣偉大。

——《塔木德》（猶太教文獻）

Whoever destroys a single life is as guilty as though he had destroyed
the entire world; and whoever rescues a single life earns as much merit
as though he had rescued the entire world.　　　　*—The Talmud*

203

衰老其實是心境上的問題。只要你不在乎年齡，
它就不會是個問題。

——薩奇‧佩吉（美國大聯盟棒球選手，1906-1982）

Age is a question of mind over matter. If you don't mind, it doesn't
matter.　　　　　　　　　　　　　　　　　—Satchel Paige

204

在所有語言和文字中，最為哀傷的莫過於：「早
知當初！」。

——約翰‧葛林里夫‧惠提爾（美國詩人，1807-1892）

For of all sad words of tongue or pen / the saddest are these; It might
have been!　　　　　　　　　　　　—John Greenleaf Whittier

205

沒有一件事是絕對真理，縱然有人願為它犧牲生命。

—— 奧斯卡・王爾德（愛爾蘭文學家，1854–1900）

A thing is not necessarily true because a man dies for it.

—Oscar Wilde

206

臉上的皺紋不過是微笑所留下的軌跡。

—— 馬克・吐溫（美國作家，1835–1910）

Wrinkles should merely indicate where smiles have been.

—Mark Twain

207

衰老不過是一種壞習慣，而勤奮的人沒有時間去養成它。

—— 安德烈・莫洛亞（法國傳記作家，1885–1967）

Growing old is no more than a bad habit which a busy person has not time to form.

—André Maurois

208

死亡之道亦為人生之道。

—— 馬可·奧里略（羅馬皇帝、哲學家，121-180 A. D.）

The act of dying is also one of the acts of life.　　　—Marcus Aurelius

209

如果你總是憂懼於災厄，災厄自會降臨。擔憂死亡，則是會加速自己的衰敗。正面且靈活地思考，佐以自信與信仰，則生活將更為穩固且充滿行動力，你也會得到更豐富的經驗與成就。

—— 史瓦米·施瓦納達（印度醫生、精神導師，1887-1963）

If you think about disaster, you will get it. Brood about death and you hasten your demise. Think positively and masterfully, with confidence and faith, and life becomes more secure, more fraught with action, richer in achievement and experience.　　　—Swami Sivananda

210

渺冥有手書天命，
且復續寫揮不停。
任君流盡目中淚，
半行一字莫能洗。

—— 奧瑪·開儼（波斯詩人、數學家、哲學家，1048-1122）

The Moving Finger writes; and having writ,
Moves on; nor all your Piety nor Wit
Shall lure it back to cancel half a Line,
Nor all your Tears wash out a Word of it.

　　　　　　　　　　　　　　—Omar Khayyam

211

所謂年老，代表的不只是白髮與皺紋，或者那
英雄遲暮、長江後浪推前浪的感慨。真正的邪
惡不在於身體的衰敗，而在於靈魂的冷漠。

—— 安德烈·莫洛亞（法國傳記作家，1885-1967）

Old age is far more than white hair, wrinkles, the feeling that it is
too late and the game finished, that the stage belongs to the rising
generations. The true evil is not the weakening of the body, but the
indifference of the soul.

　　　　　　　　　　　　　　—André Maurois

212

年輕時，如果你從馬背上摔下來，你可能只會
弄斷一條腿。如果你像我這樣的年紀，那這一
摔可能會把你全身都拆散了。

—— 羅伊・羅傑斯（美國演員，1911–1998）

When you're young and you fall off a horse, you may break something.
When you're my age and you fall off, you splatter.　　—Roy Rogers

213

當你在上帝面前接受最終裁判時，祂審度的不
是你的成功或失敗，而是你如何活過這一生。

—— 葛蘭特蘭・萊斯（美國運動專欄作家，1880–1954）

When the great scorer comes to write against your name, he marks not
that you won or lost, but how you played the game.

—Grantland Rice

214

終身的幸福！沒有任何人能夠忍受這樣的「福
份」：那將是人間地獄。

—— 蕭伯納（愛爾蘭劇作家、文學批評家，1856–1950）

A lifetime of happiness! No man alive could bear it: it would be hell on
earth.　　—George Bernard Shaw

215

年老的心智就像一匹老馬；如果想讓牠正常幹活，你就得不時地操練牠。

—— 約翰・亞當斯（美國第二任總統，1735－1826）

Old minds are like old horses; you must exercise them if you wish to keep them in working order. —John Adams

216

我過去曾虛擲光陰，而現在，光陰正掏空著我。

—— 威廉・莎士比亞（英國劇作家，1564－1616）

I wasted time, and now doth time waste me.

—William Shakespeare

217

如果能在人生的每個階段都體會到美，那你永遠都不會老。

—— 法蘭茲・卡夫卡（波希米亞德語小說家，1883－1924）

Anyone who keeps the ability to see beauty in every age of life really never grows old. —Franz Kafka

218

人生就像牌局：你手中的牌是天命注定，但是
你要如何運用這些牌，則是自由意志的發揮。

—— 賈瓦哈拉爾·尼赫魯（印度第一任總理，1889-1964）

Life is like a game of cards. The hand you are dealt is determinism; the
way you play it is free will.　　　　　　　　—Jawaharlal Nehru

219

孩子害怕黑暗是情有可原。而人生真正的悲劇，
是那些見不得光的成年人。

—— 柏拉圖（希臘哲學家，427-347 B.C.）

We can easily forgive a child who is afraid of the dark. The real tragedy
of life is when men are afraid of the light.　　　　　　　—Plato

220

每一個不曾起舞的日子，都是對生命的辜負；
每一個不帶歡笑的所謂「真理」，皆為虛妄。

—— 尼采（德國哲學家，1844-1900）

And we should consider every day lost on which we have not danced
at least once. And we should call every truth false which was not
accompanied by at least one laugh.　　　—Friedrich Wilhelm Nietzsche

221

面對外在的事物，我們所能窺見的不只是它們的本質，更是我們自己的心性。

—— 阿內絲・尼恩（法／古巴裔美國作家，1903－1977）

We don't see things as they are, we see them as we are.

—Anaïs Nin

222

真正的快樂並非是面對他人時的笑容，而是面對自己時的喜悅。

—— 馬塞爾・普魯斯特（法國作家，1871－1922）

The happy man is not he who seems thus to others, but who seems thus to himself.

—Marcel Proust

223

在你背叛朋友的同時，你也背叛了自己的信念。

—— 艾薩克・巴甚維斯・辛格
（美國猶太裔小說家，1902－1991）

When you betray somebody else, you also betray yourself.

—Isaac Bashevis Singer

224

無論當前的處境多麼黑暗，你總要抬頭看見那些永遠隱藏在其中的可能性。

—— 諾曼・文森・皮爾（美國傳教士，1898-1993）

No matter how dark things seem to be or actually are, raise your sights and see the possibilities—always see them, for they're always there.

—Norman Vincent Peale

225

如果你想要讓三個人共同保守一個秘密，就得宰掉其中兩個。

—— 班傑明・富蘭克林（美國政治家、作家，1706-1790）

In order for three people to keep a secret, two must be dead.

—Benjamin Franklin

226

在大多數心智清楚的人中，不存在著所謂性別、婚姻、或性情的問題。人生中最重要且永恆的問題是：「如何成為一個誠實的人」和「面對死亡」，其他問題在這兩者之前都是微不足道。

——G‧K‧卻斯特頓（英國作家，1874-1936）

In the majority of sane human lives there is no problem of sex at all; there is no problem of marriage at all; there is no problem of temperament at all; for all these problems are dwarfed and rendered ridiculous by the standing problem of being a moderately honest man and paying the butcher.　　　　　—G. K. Chesterton

227

午後三時是個不早不晚的尷尬時刻，要工作也是無從下手。

——尚‧保羅‧沙特（法國哲學家，1905-1980）

Three o'clock is always too late or too early for anything you want to do.
　　　　　　　　　　　　　　　　　—Jean-Paul Sartre

228

我總是懷抱希望，縱然它們並不總是會實現。

——奧維德（羅馬詩人，43 B. C. -17 A. D. ）

My hopes are not always realized, but I always hope.　　　—Ovid

229

有時候一根雪茄就只是一根雪茄，不是什麼陽具象徵——別想太多。

——席格蒙‧佛洛伊德
（奧地利精神分析師，1856-1939）

Sometimes a cigar is just a cigar.   —Sigmund Freud

230

我們所身處的是一個最好的世界，其中一切事物都是最美好的。

——伏爾泰（法國哲學家，1694-1778）

All is for the best in the best of all possible worlds.   —Voltaire

231

降臨在這土地上的一切也都同時降臨在人類身上。我們無法編織人生的網絡；我們只不過是其中的一縷絲線罷了。種下什麼因，就會得到什麼果。

——西雅圖酋長（美國印第安部落領袖，1784-1866）

Whatever befalls the earth befalls the sons and daughters of the earth. We did not weave the web of life; We are merely a strand in it. What we do with the web, we do to ourselves . . .   ——Chief Seattle

232

這個世界充滿了神奇的事物，它們正耐心地等待我們變得更睿智。

—— 伯特蘭·羅素（英國哲學家、數學家，1872-1970）

The world is full of magical things patiently waiting for our wits to grow sharper.
　　　　　　　　　　　　　　　　　　—Bertrand Russell

233

紓解憤怒的良藥就是時間。

—— 布里根姆·揚（美國摩門教領袖，1801-1877）

The best remedy for anger is delay.　　　　　　　—Brigham Young

234

好好地活下去，這就是對仇敵最大的報復。

——《塔木德》（猶太教文獻）

Live well. It is the greatest revenge.　　　　　　　—*The Talmud*

235

一艘船艦不會只拋下一支錨；人生也不該只懷抱一種希望。

—— 愛比克泰德（古羅馬斯多葛學派哲學家，50–135 A. D.）

A ship ought not to be held by one anchor, nor life by a single hope.
—Epictetus

236

我依舊懷抱著理想：因為儘管面對了這一切醜惡與恐怖，我仍然堅信人類本心的良善。

—— 安妮・法蘭克
（德國二次大戰時期日記作家，1929–1945）

I keep my ideals, because in spite of everything I still believe that people are really good at heart.
—Anne Frank

237

社會就像一艘船，船上每個人都應該要有掌舵的準備。

—— 亨里克・易卜生（挪威劇作家，1828–1906）

A community is like a ship, everyone ought to be prepared to take the helm.
—Henrik Ibsen

238

在我們的生命之火即將黯淡的時候，總會有人
吹上一口氣，使光焰重現。我們每一個人都應
該對那些重新點亮自己生命的人，懷抱最深的
感謝。

—— 阿爾伯特·史懷哲（德／法國神學家、醫學家、諾貝爾
和平獎得主，1875－1964）

Sometimes our light goes out but is blown into flame by another human
being. Each of us owes deepest thanks to those who have rekindled this
light. 　　　　　　　　　　　　　　　　　　—Albert Schweitzer

239

人生不會因為死亡而失去樂趣。同樣地，人生
的沈重也不會因為歡笑而稍稍減輕。

—— 蕭伯納（愛爾蘭劇作家、文學批評家，1856－1950）

Life does not cease to be funny when people die any more than it ceases
to be serious when people laugh. 　　　　　　　　—Bernard Shaw

240

欲望構築了一半的生命；冷漠則使人籠罩在死
亡的半邊陰影下。

—— 紀伯倫（黎巴嫩詩人，1883－1931）

Desire is half of life, indifference is half of death. 　　—Kahlil Gibran

241

生命是喜悅，死亡是平靜。一切煩惱皆來自於
兩者之間。

——以撒·艾西莫夫（俄裔美國科幻小說家，1920–1992）

Life is pleasant. Death is peaceful. It's the transition that's troublesome.
—Isaac Asimov

242

人生中最大的慰藉，就是能夠坦率直言。

——伏爾泰（法國哲學家，1694–1778）

The great consolation in life is to say what one thinks.　　—Voltaire

243

人對死亡感到恐懼，就如同孩童懼怕走入黑暗。
各式各樣以訛傳訛的故事對後者推波助瀾，對
前者亦如是。

——法蘭西斯·培根爵士
（英國哲學家、散文作家，1561–1626）

Men fear death, as children fear to go in the dark; and as that natural
fear in children is increased with tales, so is the other.
—Sir Francis Bacon

244

如果一個人無法找到他可以為之獻身的理念，
那他根本不配活著。

—— 馬丁·路德·金恩
（美國牧師、非裔美國人權運動領袖，1929－1968）

If man hasn't discovered something that he will die for, he isn't fit to
live. —Martin Luther King, Jr.

245

死亡並不會消滅光明；祂只是吹熄了一盞燈，
以迎接更燦爛的黎明。

—— 泰戈爾（印度詩人，1861－1941）

Death is not extinguishing the light; it is putting out the lamp because
dawn has come. —Rabindranath Tagore

246

對死亡感到歡欣吧！因為真理如是：沒有任何
邪惡能降臨在好人身上，活著的時候如此，死
後亦然。

—— 蘇格拉底（古希臘哲學家，469－399 B. C.）

Be of good cheer about death and know this as a truth—that no evil can
happen to a good man, either in life or after death. —Socrates

247

我向生命說道：「我想聽聽死亡如何說話。」
生命揚聲說道：「你正聽著呢。」

—— 紀伯倫（黎巴嫩詩人，1883-1931）

I said to Life, "I would hear Death speak." And Life raised her voice a little higher and said, "You hear him now." —Kahlil Gibran

248

在賽場上的騎士抵達終點之後並不會立刻停下腳步；在全然的靜止不動之前總會有一段緩步。而在人生中，這陣緩步並不僅僅指向止息，因為活著就是一段不斷衝刺的旅程。

—— 小奧利弗‧溫德爾‧霍姆斯
（美國法學家、最高法院大法官，1841-1935）

The riders in a race do not stop short when they reach the goal. There is a little finishing canter before they come to a standstill. . . . The canter that brings you to a standstill need not be only coming to rest. It cannot be while you still live. —Oliver Wendell Holmes, Jr.

249

我們對死亡的恐懼就好像我們害怕夏天太快結束一樣。但是在我們縱情享樂之後，我們總會說：「我已不虛此生」。

—— 拉爾夫·沃爾多·愛默生
（美國哲學家、詩人，1803-1882）

Our fear of death is like our fear that summer will be short, but when we have had our swing of pleasure, our fill of fruit, and our swelter of heat, we say we have had our day.　　　—Ralph Waldo Emerson

250

能夠善終的悲傷是甜美的。

—— 埃斯庫羅斯（希臘悲劇作家，525-456 B.C.）

Sweet is a grief well ended.　　　—Aeschylus

251

如果你能夠心滿意足地回首自己過去的生命，你就好像擁有兩個人生一般。

—— 紀伯倫（黎巴嫩詩人，1883-1931）

To be able to look back upon one's life in satisfaction, is to live twice.
　　　—Kahlil Gibran

252

當我活得越長，我就越能夠體會到人生之美。

—— 法蘭克・洛伊・萊特（美國建築家，1869-1959）

The longer I live, the more beautiful life becomes.

—Frank Lloyd Wright

253

比賽在最後一個出局數出現前，都還不算是真正結束。

—— 尤吉・貝拉（前美國大聯盟棒球員，1925-2015）

It's not over until it's over.

—Yogi Berra

254

當我回首那些曾經使我苦惱的憂慮時，我想起了一個故事：一位長者在臨終前談到他一生中的許多煩惱，而這些煩惱大多從未發生過。

—— 溫斯頓・邱吉爾（前英國首相，1874-1965）

When I look back on all these worries, I remember the story of the old man who said on his deathbed that he had had a lot of trouble in his life, most of which had never happened.

—Sir Winston Churchill

255

無論烈火或狂風、生命或死亡，皆無法磨滅我
們的善舉。

—— 釋迦牟尼（佛教創始者，563－483 B.C.）

Neither fire nor wind, birth nor death can erase our good deeds.

—Buddha

256

死亡終結生命，但不會終結人與人之間的羈絆。

—— 傑克·李蒙（美國演員，1925－2001）

Death ends a life, not a relationship.

—Jack Lemmon

257

我拒絕接受世界末日這樣的論調；我認為人類
會憑藉著毅力而世世代代地延續下去。即使最
後的喪鐘於落日餘暉中、海邊孤崖畔響起，我
仍舊能夠聽見人類弱而不衰的低語聲。我相信
人類不但能夠堅忍，更終將克服一切。而人類
能夠永恆地存續下去，不只是因為在萬物之中
獨有綿延不斷的話語，更是因為人類擁有高貴
的靈魂、同情心，以及犧牲奉獻的精神。

—— 威廉·福克納（美國小說家，1897-1962）

I decline to accept the end of man. It is easy enough to say that man is
immortal because he will endure: that when the last ding-dong of doom
has clanged and faded from the last worthless rock hanging tideless in
the last red and dying evening, that even then there will still be one
more sound: that of his puny inexhaustible voice, still talking. I refuse to
accept this. I believe that man will not merely endure: he will prevail. He
is immortal, not because he alone among creatures has an inexhaustible
voice, but because he has a soul, a spirit capable of compassion and
sacrifice and endurance.
—William Faulkner

258

別對未來感到恐懼，也切莫對過去感到憂傷。

—— 雪萊（英國詩人，1792-1822）

Fear not for the future, weep not for the past.

—Percy Bysshe Shelley

259

我並非是興之所至地說真話，而是在當說之際以勇氣道出真相。隨著成長，我對於真理的勇氣也逐漸地增長。

——米歇爾‧德‧蒙田（法國散文家，1533－1592）

I speak truth, not so much as I would, but as much as I dare; and I dare a little more, as I grow older.　　　——Michel de Montaigne

260

我永遠記得在亞利桑納州墓園中的一個碑文：「這裡安息著傑克‧威廉斯，他已經盡了他最大的努力。」我想這是一個人所能擁有的最佳墓誌銘。

——杜魯門（美國第三十三任總統，1884－1972）

I always remember an epitaph which is in the cemetery at Tombstone, Arizona. It says: "Here lies Jack Williams. He done his damnedest." I think that is the greatest epitaph a man can have.　　——Harry S. Truman

261

善待幼者、憐憫長者、對辛勤努力的人感同身受、無論面對柔弱或強悍，都以寬容待之。唯有如此，你才能擁有長遠的人生，因為以上種種角色你都將在人生中扮演到。

—— 喬治・華盛頓・卡弗
（美國農業化學家、發明家，1864－1943）

How far you go in life depends on your being tender with the young, compassionate with the aged, sympathetic with the striving, and tolerant of the weak and strong. Because someday in your life you will have been all of these. —George Washington Carver

262

在終局到來時，一切事物都不過是個好玩的玩笑。

—— 卓別林（英國喜劇演員，1889－1977）

In the end, everything is a gag. —Charlie Chaplin

第二章
愛與友情

CHAPTER 2
Love and Friendship

263

何謂朋友？就是一個分居在兩個軀體內的靈魂。

—— 亞里斯多德（希臘哲學家，384－322 B.C.）

What is a friend? A single soul dwelling in two bodies.　　　—Aristotle

264

在你認為你已經展現出必要的善意的時候，總要想想也許你可以做得更多。

—— 詹姆斯·馬修·巴里爵士（英國作家，1860－1937）

Always be a little kinder than necessary.　　—Sir James Matthew Barrie

265

人類總是不講道理、沒有邏輯且自我中心。縱使如此，還是當以愛包容。

—— 德蕾莎修女（阿爾巴尼亞裔印度修女、諾貝爾
和平獎得主，1910－1997）

People are unreasonable, illogical, and self-centered. Love them anyway.
　　—Mother Teresa

266

犯錯乃人之常情；寬恕則使人超凡入聖。

—— 亞歷山大‧波普（英國詩人、諷刺文學家，1688-1744）

To err is human, to forgive divine.　　　　　　—Alexander Pope

267

犯錯乃人之常情；寬恕則不是那麼常見。

—— 法蘭克林‧亞當斯（美國專欄作家，1881-1960）

To err is human; to forgive, infrequent.　　　　—Franklin P. Adams

268

從一個人所喜愛的事物，就能窺見他的品格。

—— 索爾‧貝婁（美國小說家，1915-2005）

A person is only as good as what they love.　　　　—Saul Bellow

269

而到了最後，你所得到的愛，不多不少就是你
所曾經付出的愛。

—— 保羅・麥卡尼
（英國歌手、作詞家、披頭四成員，1942-）

And in the end, the love you take is equal to the love you make.
—Paul McCartney

270

真正的友誼就是能夠互相交換誠心的建議。

—— 西塞羅
（羅馬雄辯家、哲學家、作家，106-43 B. C.）

To give counsel as well as to take it is a feature of true friendship.
—Marcus Tullius Cicero

271

一根蠟燭能夠點燃千千萬萬根其他的蠟燭，而
它的壽命並不會因此而縮短。同樣地，幸福也
並不會因為分享而減少。

—— 釋迦牟尼（佛教創始者，563-483 B. C.）

Thousands of candles can be lighted from a single candle, And the life
of the candle will not be shortened. Happiness never decreases by being
shared.
—Buddha

272

仁愛之心勝過一切冠冕；單純信念比貴族血統
更為高尚。

—— 阿佛烈‧丁尼生 (英國詩人，1809-1892)

Kind hearts are more than coronets / And simple faith than Norman
blood.　　　　　　　　　　　　　　　—Alfred, Lord Tennyson

273

歡笑聲能夠縮短人與人之間的距離。

—— 維克托‧伯厄 (丹麥幽默作家、鋼琴家，1909-2000)

Laughter is the closest distance between two people.　　—Victor Borge

274

一顆心縱使碎了，它也還是會如常地跳動下去。

—— 芬妮‧傅雷格 (美國演員、作者，1944-)

A heart can be broken, but it will keep beating just the same.

　　　　　　　　　　　　　　　　　　　　—Fannie Flagg

275

戀愛就好像戰爭一樣：輕易地被挑起，卻難以
結束。

——H·L·孟肯（美國編輯、評論家，1880-1956）

Love is like war; easy to begin but very hard to stop.　—H. L. Mencken

276

在你評斷一位朋友的時候，最好記住他也正用
同樣神聖且超然的公正態度審視著你。

——阿諾德·貝內特（英國小說家，1867-1931）

It is well, when judging a friend, to remember that he is judging you
with the same godlike and superior impartiality.

—Arnold Bennett

277

縱然遭遇了心碎之事，世界還是會照常運轉。

——馬可·奧里略（羅馬皇帝、哲學家，121-180 A. D.）

Though you break your heart, men will go on as before.

—Marcus Aurelius

278

當我的靈魂想起我的好朋友們時，再也沒有比
這更快樂的時刻了。

　　　── 威廉·莎士比亞（英國劇作家，1564-1616）

I count myself in nothing else so happy / As in a soul rememb'ring my
good friends. 　　　　　　　　　　　　　—William Shakespeare

279

人類情感自有其邏輯，而那是理性所不能夠理
解的。

　　　　　　　── 帕斯卡（法國哲學家，1623-1662）

The heart has its reasons of which reason knows nothing.
　　　　　　　　　　　　　　　　　　　—Blaise Pascal

280

要有一顆永遠柔軟的心、永不厭倦的性情，以
及一種不會傷人或自傷的風格。

　　　── 查爾斯·狄更斯（英國小說家，1812-1870）

Have a heart that never hardens, a temper that never tires, a touch that
never hurts. 　　　　　　　　　　　　　　—Charles Dickens

281

能夠不帶任何嫉妒地向朋友的成就致敬，是極少數人能夠擁有的天賦。

—— 埃斯庫羅斯（希臘悲劇作家，525-456 B.C.）

Few men have the natural strength to honour a friend's success without envy. —Aeschylus

282

能感受到愉悅，就是一件了不起的事。

—— 查爾斯・狄更斯（英國小說家，1812-1870）

There might be some credit in being jolly. —Charles Dickens

283

說出善意的言語並不需要什麼代價。它們並不會使你的唇舌受到傷害。它們會讓聽者也同樣心懷善念，並且在人心中刻畫下美麗的形象。

—— 帕斯卡（法國哲學家，1623-1662）

Kind words do not cost much. They never blister the tongue or lips. They make other people good-natured. They also produce their own image on men's souls, and a beautiful image it is. —Blaise Pascal

284

一件帶給別人快樂的善舉，勝過千萬次膜拜和
祈禱。

——甘地（印度民族主義領袖，1869-1948）

To give pleasure to a single heart by a single kind act is better than a
thousand head-bowings in prayer. ——Mohandas Gandhi

285

善良並不一定存在於偉大之中，但偉大必定存
在於善良之中。

—— 阿特納奧斯（希臘修辭學家，生卒年不詳，活躍於西元
二世紀左右）

Goodness does not consist in greatness, but greatness in goodness.
——Athenaeus

286

當繁星為我們燃放著熱情，
而我們卻無法回應時，我們該如何自處？
倘若人們無法以相等的情感對待彼此，
就讓我成為那個愛得更多一些的人吧。

———W·H·奧登（英裔美籍詩人，1907-1973）

How should we like it were stars to burn
With a passion for us, we could not return?
If equal affection cannot be,
Let the more loving one be me. ———W. H. Auden

287

愛，就是一位偉大的藝術家。

——— 露意莎·奧爾柯特（美國小說家，1832-1888）

Love is a great beautifier. ———Louisa May Alcott

288

將你唯一的微笑留給你所愛的人吧。別在家裡陰沈著一張臉，卻在街上對陌生人笑容可掬地道早安。

——馬婭・安傑盧（美國詩人、人權運動者，1928–2014）

If you have only one smile in you, give it to the people you love.
Don't be surly at home, then go out in the street and start grinning "Good morning" at total strangers.　　　　　——Maya Angelou

289

一個人倘若沒有朋友，縱然擁有家財萬貫，他也會沒有活下去的動力。

——亞里斯多德（希臘哲學家，384–322 B.C.）

Without friends no one would choose to live, though he had all other goods.　　　　　——Aristotle

290

一個心懷邪念的朋友，要比野獸更令人恐懼。
後者也許會傷害你的身體，前者卻毒害你的心
靈。

—— 釋迦牟尼（佛教創始者，563-483 B. C.）

An insincere and evil friend is more to be feared than a wild beast; a wild beast may wound your body, but an evil friend will wound your mind.

—Buddha

291

生活富足且身強體壯皆是福氣，但是能與許多
朋友相交，更是快意之事。

—— 歐里庇得斯（希臘劇作家，480-406 B. C.）

It is a good thing to be rich and a good thing to be strong, but it is a better thing to be loved by many friends.　　　　—Euripides

292

逝去的友誼總是讓人傷感。

—— 亨利・羅林斯（美國歌手，1961-）

It's sad when someone you know becomes someone you knew.

—Henry Rollins

293

在初次認識的當下，真正的朋友就能夠與你相知相惜。而點頭之交就算花上一輩子也無法做到。

—— 李察‧巴赫（美國作家，1936-）

Your friends will know you better in the first moment you meet than your acquaintants will know you in a lifetime.　　—Richard Bach

294

唯有寬恕才能夠使我們得到救贖。

—— 亞西西的聖方濟（義大利神父，1182-1226）

It is in pardoning that we are pardoned.　　—Saint Francis of Assisi

295

在我所仰慕的人們之中，我並沒看到任何共同之處。但在我所愛的人們之中，我發現他們都能使我歡笑。

—— W‧H‧奧登（英裔美籍詩人，1907-1973）

In those whom I like, I can find no common denominator; in those whom I love I can: they all make me laugh.　　—W. H. Auden

296

那些能夠帶給他人溫暖的人，自己的生命也將
充滿陽光。

—— 詹姆斯・馬修・巴里爵士（英國作家，1860-1937）

Those who bring sunshine to the lives of others cannot keep it from
themselves. —Sir James Matthew Barrie

297

離群索居，決不可能成為成功的人。倘若無法
與其他心靈對話，孤獨之人的心靈將會逐漸枯
萎；他將只能聽著自己思想的回音，而得不到
任何啟發。

—— 賽珍珠（美國小說家，1892-1973）

The person who tries to live alone will not succeed as a human being.
His heart withers if it does not answer another heart. His mind shrinks
away if he hears only the echoes of his own thoughts and finds no other
inspiration. —Pearl Buck

298

友誼的最佳明證，就在於能夠委婉地指出朋友
的過錯。而更為可貴的，就是懷著感激之情接
受朋友的指正，並且改正錯誤。

——愛德華・鮑沃爾利頓
（英國小說家、詩人，1803－1873）

One of the surest evidences of friendship that one individual can display
to another is telling him gently of a fault. If any other can excel it, it is
listening to such a disclosure with gratitude, and amending the error.

——Edward Bulwer-Lytton

299

朋友之間不該過度依賴；沒有人能夠在庇蔭中
成長。

——里歐・布斯卡里亞
（美國教育家、作家，1924－1998）

Don't smother each other. No one can grow in the shade.

——Leo Buscaglia

300

友情帶來最大的寬解與慰藉，因為一切都無需解釋。

—— 凱瑟琳·曼斯菲爾德（紐西蘭作家，1888－1923）

I always felt that the great high privilege, relief and comfort of friendship was that one had to explain nothing. —Katherine Mansfield

301

友情就像金錢，賺來容易守成難。

—— 塞繆爾·巴特勒（英國詩人、作家，1612－1680）

Friendship is like money, easier made than kept. —Samuel Butler

302

如果你能慷慨地分享你的喜悅與成就，你就能夠獲得寬恕。

—— 卡繆（法國存在主義哲學家，1913－1960）

You are forgiven for your happiness and your successes only if you generously consent to share them. —Albert Camus

303

愛是一種無可抑制的欲望：欲望著有人會無可抑制地愛上你。

—— 羅伯特·佛洛斯特（美國詩人，1874-1963）

Love is an irresistible desire to be irresistibly desired.　—Robert Frost

304

如果你想要贏得朋友，最重要的就是記住他們。如果你記得我的名字，就是對我的一個細微的讚美；這代表著我使你留下了些許印象。記得我的名字，這就使我感受到尊重。

—— 戴爾·卡內基
（美國人際關係學家、作家，1888-1955）

If you want to win friends, make it a point to remember them. If you remember my name, you pay me a subtle compliment; you indicate that I have made an impression on you. Remember my name and you add to my feeling of importance.　—Dale Carnegie

305

如果你能夠在一個擁有偉大心靈的人身邊挺
立，應該在他心中留下自己的好印象。如果在
你身旁的是一個心胸狹窄的人，就讓他沾沾自
喜於自己的形象吧。

—— 塞繆爾‧泰勒‧柯勒律治（英國詩人，1772-1834）

If you would stand well with a great mind, leave him with a favorable
impression of yourself; if with a little mind, leave him with a favorable
impression of himself.　　　　　　　　—Samuel Taylor Coleridge

306

若要評斷一個人，當審視其與何人為敵、與何
人為友。

—— 約瑟夫‧康拉德（英國小說家，1857-1924）

You shall judge a man by his foes as well as by his friends.
　　　　　　　　　　　　　　　　　　　—Joseph Conrad

307

老柴好燒；老馬好騎；老書好讀；老酒好飲——
而老朋友最值得信任。

——法蘭西斯·培根爵士
（英國哲學家、散文作家，1561-1626）

As old wood is best to burn; old horses to ride; old books to read; old
wine to drink; so are old friends most trusty to use.

—Sir Francis Bacon

308

朋友給的建議就好像陰晴不定的天氣，時好時
壞。

——佚名

Advice from your friends is like the weather, some of it is good, some of
it is bad.　　　　　　　　　　　　　　　　　—Anonymous

309

朋友是一個我能夠真實以對的人。在他面前，
我能夠說出內心的一切。

——拉爾夫·沃爾多·愛默生
（美國哲學家、詩人，1803-1882）

A friend is a person with whom I may be sincere. Before him, I may
think aloud.　　　　　　　　　　　　　　—Ralph Waldo Emerson

310

一顆能愛人的心，代表著最真實的智慧。

—— 查爾斯·狄更斯（英國小說家，1812-1870）

A loving heart is the truest wisdom.　　　　　—Charles Dickens

311

若我能挽救一顆即將破碎的心，或緩解一陣苦痛，那我已然不虛此生。

—— 艾蜜莉·狄瑾孫（美國詩人，1830-1886）

If I can stop one heart from breaking, If I can ease one pain,
Then my life will not have been in vain.　　—Emily Elizabeth Dickinson

312

友情的榮光，並不在於那緊握的雙手、和善的微笑或相伴的喜悅。而是在於你發現有人能夠全心全意地信任你的那一瞬間，所激發的心靈昇華。

—— 拉爾夫·沃爾多·愛默生
（美國哲學家、詩人，1803-1882）

The glory of friendship is not the outstretched hand, nor the kindly smile, nor the joy of companionship; it is the spiritual inspiration that comes to one when you discover that someone else believes in you and is willing to trust you with a friendship.　　—Ralph Waldo Emerson

313

一個在戀愛中的人跟瘋子沒什麼兩樣。

　　── 席格蒙・佛洛伊德（奧地利精神分析師，1856－1939）

One is very crazy when in love.　　　　　　　　　　　—Sigmund Freud

314

愛的本質就是精神上的烈焰。

　　　　　　　　　　　　　　　── 伊曼紐・斯威登堡
　　　　　　　　　　　　　　（瑞典宗教哲學家，1688－1772）

Love in its essence is spiritual fire.　　　　　—Emanuel Swedenborg

315

愛，就是人心上的缺口。

　　── 班・赫克特（美國劇作家、導演，1894－1964）

Love is a hole in the heart.　　　　　　　　　　　　—Ben Hecht

316

啊，何時人心才能明瞭：
順應事物的滄海桑田、
不失優雅與理性的退讓、
以及低頭接受一段愛情
或美好季節的結束，
並非是背叛自己本心的罪行？

——羅伯特・佛洛斯特（美國詩人，1874－1963）

Ah, when to the heart of man
Was it ever less than a treason
To go with the drift of things
To yield with a grace to reason
And bow and accept at the end
Of a love or a season.

——Robert Frost

317

滿上彼此的杯盞,但切莫只從一盞中取飲。
分享彼此的麵包,但切莫只從同一塊取食。
縱情共舞與同聲高歌,但也保持自身的獨立;
魯特琴弦根根分離,縱然它們同為一首歌而震
動。

—— 紀伯倫(黎巴嫩詩人,1883-1931)

Fill each other's cup but drink not from one cup.
Give one another of your bread but eat not from the same loaf.
Sing and dance together and be joyous, but let each one of you be alone,
Even as the strings of a lute are alone though they quiver with the same
music.
—Kahlil Gibran

318

擁有一位真正的朋友就是最大的福氣,而我們
無須為得到這樣的福氣費盡心機。

—— 法蘭索瓦·德·拉羅希福可
(法國作家,1613-1680)

A true friend is the greatest of all blessings, and that which we take the
least care of all to acquire.
—François de La Rochefoucauld

319

當你很驚訝地對一個人說：「什麼！你也是這樣認為的嗎？我以為只有我一個人有這樣的想法。」的時候，友情就此誕生。

——C·S·路易斯（英國作家，1898-1963）

Friendship is born at that moment when one person says to another: What! You, too? I thought I was the only one.　　　　——C. S. Lewis

320

我們必須建立並保有寬恕的能力。無法寬恕也代表著無法去愛人。就算在最邪惡的人心中也是會有一絲善良；而在最善良的人心中也存在著些許邪惡。

——馬丁·路德·金恩
（美國牧師、非裔美國人權運動領袖，1929-1968）

We must develop and maintain the capacity to forgive. He who is devoid of the power to forgive is devoid of the power to love. There is some good in the worst of us and some evil in the best of us.
　　　　——Martin Luther King, Jr.

321

愛情乃是以天性為畫布，由想像力揮灑色彩的油畫。

—— 伏爾泰（法國哲學家，1694－1778）

Love is a canvas furnished by Nature and embroidered by imagination.
　　　　　　　—Voltaire

322

戀愛時，我們所愛的是人，而不是他的優點。有時候我們反而會因他的缺陷而愛他。

—— 雅克・馬里頓（法國天主教哲學家，1882－1973）

We don't love qualities, we love persons; sometimes by reason of their defects as well as of their qualities.　　　—Jacques Maritain

323

我能夠為朋友做到的很簡單，就是做他的朋友。

—— 亨利・大衛・梭羅
（美國作家、自然主義者，1817－1862）

The most I can do for my friend is simply to be his friend.
　　　　　　　—Henry David Thoreau

324

傾聽是一種富有魅力且奇異的特質，甚至是一種創造性的力量。那些能夠傾聽的朋友吸引著我們。傾聽使我們揭露並詳述事實，也重新塑造了我們。

——卡爾·奧古特斯·曼尼哲
（美國精神科醫師，1893–1990）

Listening is a magnetic and strange thing, a creative force. The friends who listen to us are the ones we move toward. When we are listened to, it creates us, makes us unfold and expand.

——Dr. Karl Augustus Menninger

325

許多人們共通的毛病就好像臥房的拖鞋一樣舒服，使人很容易就陷入其中。

——菲莉絲·麥克金利（美國詩人，1905–1961）

Faults shared are as comfortable as bedroom slippers and as easy to slip into.

——Phyllis McGinley

326

我已經體會到：若能與我喜愛的人相處，則人生足矣。

——華特・惠特曼（美國詩人，1819－1892）

I have learned that to be with those I like is enough.

——Walt Whitman

327

用雙臂緊緊地抱住你真正的朋友。

——尼采（德國哲學家，1844－1900）

Hold a true friend with both your hands.

——Friedrich Wilhelm Nietzsche

328

離別對於愛情來說，就好似風對於火一般。它吹熄了小小的火苗，但卻助長了更燦爛的光焰。

——羅傑・德・哈布丁・畢西伯爵
（法國諷刺作家，1618－1693）

Absence is to love what wind is to fire; it extinguishes the small, it enkindles the great.

——Comte Roger de Bussy-Rabutin

329

一個吻,乃是給愛情的玫瑰色點綴。

—— 西哈諾·貝傑哈克

(法國小說家、劇作家,1619-1655)

A kiss is a rosy dot over the "i" of loving. —Cyrano de Bergerac

330

年輕的情人會說:「我愛你,因為我需要你」。
而成熟的情人則是說:「我需要你,只因我愛
你」。

—— 埃里希·弗洛姆 (德國精神分析師,1900-1980)

Immature love says: "I love you because I need you." Mature love says "I need you because I love you." —Erich Fromm

331

一段真正的友情就好像身體的健康;我們在失
去它之前都鮮少注意到其價值。

—— 查爾斯·卡利伯·科爾頓

(英國神職人員、作家,1780-1832)

True friendship is like sound health; the value of it is seldom known until it be lost. —Charles Caleb Colton

332

一位真正的朋友，就是當全世界都離你而去時，
依舊留在你身邊的人。

—— 佚名

A real friend is one who walks in when the rest of the world walks out.

—Anonymous

333

別走在我前頭，因為我不願追隨任何人。也別
走在我背後，因為我不願引導任何人。走在我
身畔與我並進、做我的朋友吧。

—— 卡繆（法國存在主義哲學家，1913-1960）

Don't walk in front of me, I may not follow. Don't walk behind me, I may not lead. Walk beside me and be my friend.

—Albert Camus

334

人性之中最為深刻的本質，就是受人賞識的渴
望。

—— 威廉·詹姆斯
（美國心理學家、哲學家，1842-1910）

The deepest principle in human nature is the craving to be appreciated.

—William James

335

不忘久德，不思久怨。

—— 孔子（中國哲學家，551-479 B.C.）

Forget injuries, never forget kindnesses.　　　　　—Confucius

336

善良要比智慧更為重要。而認識到這一點，就
是智慧的開端。

—— 西奧多‧艾薩克‧魯賓
（美國精神科醫師、作家，1923-）

Kindness is more important than wisdom, and the recognition of this is
the beginning of wisdom.　　　　　—Theodore Isaac Rubin

337

告訴我你的朋友們都是誰，我就能夠告訴你，
你是個什麼樣的人。

—— 俄羅斯諺語

Tell me who your friends are and I will tell you who you are.
　　　　　—Russian proverb

338

莫讓我對兩顆真心的結合

承認阻礙：愛不是愛，若順應潮流而改變；

或面臨強權而屈服。

不，愛是那永恆堅定的火光，

面對風暴亦毫不動搖；愛是每艘迷航船隻的明

星，其高可望，然其價莫測。

愛不受時間的愚弄，縱然紅唇粉頰

注定受歲月的鐮刀摧殘。

愛不隨著時時刻刻而變動，而是永存以至末日。

如果有人能證明我所言為虛，就當我從未寫過

此詩，而人們則從未愛過。

（十四行詩第 116 首）

　　　　── 威廉·莎士比亞（英國劇作家，1564-1616）

Let me not to the marriage of true minds

Admit impediments. Love is not love

Which alters when it alteration finds,

Or bends with the remover to remove.

O, no! It is an ever-fixed mark

That looks on tempests and is never shaken;

It is the star to every wand'ring bark,

Whose worth's unknown, although his height be taken.

Love's not Time's fool, though rosy lips and cheeks

Within his ending sickle's compass come;

Love alters not with his brief hours and weeks,

But bears it out even to the edge of doom.

If this be error and upon me proved,

I never writ, nor no man ever loved.

　　　　　　　　　　　　　—William Shakespeare, Sonnet 116

339

愛能為一些尋常的舉止帶來非凡的美感。

—— 雪萊（英國詩人，1792-1822）

Familiar acts are beautiful through love.　　—Percy Bysshe Shelley

340

孤身一人的智慧是永遠不足的。

—— 普勞圖斯（羅馬喜劇作家，254-184 B.C.）

No man is wise enough by himself.　　　　　　—Plautus

341

結交一個朋友，就是給自己的最好禮物。

—— 羅伯特・路易斯・史蒂文生
（英國小說家，1850-1894）

A friend is a present you give yourself.

—Robert Louis Stevenson

342

一位真正的朋友能夠唱出你自己都遺忘已久的
心靈之歌。

——佚名

A friend is someone who can sing you the song of your heart when
you've forgotten it. ——Anonymous

343

除了分享你的財富給他人之外，你能做的還有
向他揭露他自身所擁有的財富。這才是最了不
起的事。

—— 班傑明·狄斯雷利（英國前首相、作家，1804-1881）

The greatest good you can do for another is not just to share your riches
but to reveal to him his own. ——Benjamin Disraeli

344

你若能夠愛過，縱然最後失去所愛，
你依舊是勝過了那些從未愛過的人。

—— 阿佛烈·丁尼生（英國詩人，1809-1892）

Tis better to have loved and lost / Than never to have loved at all.
——Alfred, Lord Tennyson

345

我們無法總是成就偉大的事，但是我們能夠以偉大的愛去成就一些平凡的事。

——德蕾莎修女

（阿爾巴尼亞裔印度修女、諾貝爾和平獎得主，1910-1997）

We cannot all do great things, but we can do small things with great love. —Mother Teresa

346

成功的愛情，是世界上最了不起的事。而失敗的愛情僅次於此。

—— 威廉·梅克比斯·薩克萊（英國小說家，1811-1863）

To love and win is the best thing. To love and lose, the next best. —William Makepeace Thackeray

347

我的朋友乃是那些對我有真正理解，並以此理解相待的人。

——亨利·大衛·梭羅

（美國作家、自然主義者，1817-1862）

My friend is one who takes me for what I am. —Henry David Thoreau

第三章
成功之道

CHAPTER 3

Success

348

逆境可以造就一個男人，而昌順的生活只會養出怪物。

——維克多・雨果
（法國小說家、詩人、劇作家，1802-1885）

Adversity makes men, and prosperity makes monsters.

——Victor Hugo

349

所謂成功，就是從一個失敗走過另一個失敗，而熱情絲毫不損。

——溫斯頓・邱吉爾（前英國首相，1874-1965）

Success is the ability to go from one failure to another with no loss of enthusiasm.

——Sir Winston Churchill

350

障礙即道路。

——禪學諺語

The obstacle is the path.

——Zen aphorism

351

你的頭裡自有腦
鞋裡自有腳
你當有自己選擇的方向
你獨自一人，且你理解自己所知
你就是引領自己人生道路的那個人。

——希奧多·蓋索

（筆名蘇斯博士，美國漫畫家，1904-1991）

You have brains in your head
You have feet in your shoes
You can steer yourself
any direction you choose
You're on your own. And you know what you know.
And YOU are the guy who'll decide where to go.

—Dr. Seuss (Theodore Geisel)

352

天才是一分的天份和九十九分的努力。

——湯瑪斯·愛迪生（美國發明家，1847-1931）

Genius is one percent inspiration and ninety-nine percent perspiration.

—Thomas Alva Edison

353

光是忙碌是不夠的，真正的問題在於：你究竟是在忙些什麼？

—— 亨利・大衛・梭羅
（美國作家、自然主義者，1817-1862）

It is not enough to be busy. . . . The question is: what are we busy about?
—Henry David Thoreau

354

人生中，如果你想要得到你所想要的事物，不可或缺的第一步就是明瞭自己的渴望。

—— 本・斯泰因（美國作家、節目主持人，1944-）

The indispensable first step to getting the things you want out of life is this: Decide what you want.
—Ben Stein

355

所有存在於世上的美好事物，都是人類原創力的果實。

—— 約翰・史都華・彌爾
（英國哲學家、政治經濟學家，1806-1873）

All good things which exist are the fruits of originality.
—John Stuart Mill

356

在人生中取得成功的人，總是能夠清楚地看見
自己的目標，並且毫不動搖地追求它。

—— 西席·地密爾（美國導演、製片人，1881-1959）

The person who makes a success of living is the one who sees his goal
steadily and aims for it unswervingly. —Cecil B. DeMille

357

實現夢想的最好方法，就是從夢想中警醒。

—— 保羅·瓦勒里（法國作家、詩人，1871-1945）

The best way to make your dreams come true is to wake up.
—Paul Valéry

358

在注重觀察的科學領域中，機遇只會對有準備
的人微笑。

—— 路易·巴斯德（法國微生物學家，1822-1895）

In the field of observation, chance favors the prepared mind.
—Louis Pasteur

359

未來屬於那些堅信自己夢想之美的人。

—— 愛蓮娜·羅斯福

（前美國第一夫人、外交官，1884-1962）

The future belongs to those who believe in the beauty of their dreams.

—Eleanor Roosevelt

360

任何事情的結果，對於那些最能夠順應時勢的人來說，都是有利的。

—— 約翰·R·伍登（美國大學籃球教練，1910-2010）

Things turn out best for the people who make the best of the way things turn out.　　　　　　—John R. Wooden

361

當你專注於將每件事情做對，或做得更好，就會發揮出無盡的創造力。

—— 約翰·厄普代克（美國小說家，1932-2009）

Any activity becomes creative when the doer cares about doing it right, or better.　　　　　　—John Updike

362

若你能夠做到展現自我，你就已成功了八成。

—— 伍迪·艾倫（美國導演、編劇、演員，1935-）

Eighty percent of success is just showing up.

—Woody Allen

363

如果你能的話，盡量使自己比別人聰明。但是記得要低調地做到。

—— 菲力·史丹何普·切斯特菲伯爵
（英國作家、政治家，1694-1773）

Be wiser than other people, if you can; but do not tell them so.

—Philip Dormer Stanhope, Lord Chesterfield

364

最嚴重的錯誤認知，就是以為成功和金錢能夠使你免於所有人生的不順遂。

—— 賴瑞·麥可莫特瑞（美國作家，1936-）

No illusion is more crucial than the illusion that great success and huge money buy you immunity from the common ills of mankind, such as cars that won't start.

—Larry McMurtry

365

當你陷入懷疑時，試著看到對你有利的一面吧。

—— 艾德蒙・霍伊爾（英國作家，1672-1769）

When in doubt, win the trick. —Edmond Hoyle

366

我們只有一個老闆，那就是顧客。他們能夠讓
公司任何一個人丟掉飯碗 —— 如果他們都選擇
在別處花錢的話。

—— 山姆・沃爾頓（美國商業大亨，1918-1992）

There is only one boss: the customer. And he can fire everybody in the
company, from the chairman on down, simply by spending his money
somewhere else. —Sam Walton

367

死亡的降臨，若不是現在，就是將來；若不是
將來，就是現在。我們所能做的，就只是做好
準備而已。

—— 威廉・莎士比亞（英國劇作家，1564-1616）

If it be now, 'tis not to come; if it be not to come, it will be now; if it be
not now, yet it will come: the readiness is all.

—William Shakespeare

368

管理球隊的成功秘訣就在於，把討厭你的五個人，跟還沒決定是否要討厭你的剩下四個人隔開來。

—— 查爾斯·凱西·史丹哲爾
（美國前大聯盟選手、球隊經理，1890－1975）

The secret of successful managing is to keep the five guys who hate you away from the four guys who haven't made up their minds.

—Charles "Casey" Stengel

369

下刀前多量幾次：三思而後行。

—— 工匠諺語

Measure twice, cut once.　　　　　　—Craftsman's aphorism

370

在審度時勢之後的冒險，與莽撞完全不同。

—— 喬治·巴頓（美國將軍，1885－1945）

Take calculated risks. That is quite different from being rash.

—George Smith Patton, Jr.

371

當我閱讀那些偉大人物的傳記時，我發現他們在贏得的第一場勝利中，所戰勝的對手就是自己。自我要求和自我節制，是一切成功的開端。

—— 杜魯門（美國第三十三任總統，1884 - 1972）

In reading the lives of great men, I found that the first victory they won was over themselves. . . . self-discipline with all of them came first.

—Harry S. Truman

372

永遠都不要輕視自己，這是一個人永遠都不該犯的錯誤。因為別人會以你看待自己的態度來評斷你。

—— 安東尼・特洛勒普（英國小說家，1815 - 1882）

Never think that you're not good enough yourself. A man should never think that. People will take you very much at your own reckoning.

—Anthony Trollope

373

人生的目標只有兩個：第一，得到你所想要的事物；第二，在得到了之後好好享受它們。而只有最睿智的人才做得到第二點。

　——羅根・皮爾薩爾・史密斯（美國散文家，1865－1946）

There are two things to aim at in life: first, to get what you want; and, after that, to enjoy it. Only the wisest of mankind achieve the second.

　　　　　　　　　　　　　　　　—Logan Pearsall Smith

374

我們必須從他人的錯誤中學習。人生苦短，你可不能將生命浪費在那些過錯上。

　——海曼・喬治・李高佛（美國將軍，1900－1986）

It is necessary for us to learn from others' mistakes. You will not live long enough to make them all yourself.　　—Hyman George Rickover

375

智者僅僅看見他所應該看見的，而非將所有能見之事物盡收眼底。

　——米歇爾・德・蒙田（法國散文家，1533－1592）

A wise man sees as much as he ought, not as much as he can.

　　　　　　　　　　　　　　　　—Michel de Montaigne

376

如果沒有了想像力與夢想的馳騁，我們就喪失了邁向無限可能的動力。夢想，其實也正是一種形式的計畫。

—— 格洛麗亞・斯泰納姆
（美國女性主義作家、記者，1934-）

Without leaps of imagination, or dreaming, we lose the excitement of possibilities. Dreaming, after all, is a form of planning.

—Gloria Steinem

377

一個努力修飾自己以迎合別人的人，終會將其自我消磨殆盡。

—— 查爾斯・舒瓦伯（美國企業家、慈善家，1937-）

The man who trims himself to suit everybody will soon whittle himself away.

—Charles Schwab

378

無事可做，就是人生最可怕的負擔。

—— 尼古拉・布瓦洛（法國詩人、文學批評家，1636-1711）

The dreadful burden of having nothing to do.

—Nicolas Boileau

379

有些人認為堅忍不拔是強大力量的展現。然而，
有些時候我們也需要同樣強大的力量去體會到
不再堅持的必要，並且毅然地放手。

—— 安·蘭德斯（當代美國專欄作家筆名，生平不詳）

Some people believe that holding on and hanging in there are signs
of great strength. However, there are times when it takes much more
strength to know when to let go—and then do it.

—Ann Landers

380

對我們大部份人來說，真正的危險不在於設定
過高的目標，然後無法達到。而是在於設定並
達到一個過低的目標，並且自滿於此。

—— 米開朗基羅（義大利文藝復興時期藝術家，1475－1564）

The greater danger for most of us lies not in setting our aim too high
and falling short, but in setting our aim too low, and achieving our
mark.

—Michelangelo

381

無聊的解藥是好奇心，而好奇心則是無藥可救的。

—— 桃樂絲・帕克（美國詩人、作家，1893-1967）

The cure for boredom is curiosity. There is no cure for curiosity.

—Dorothy Parker

382

如果對於自我有著很高的要求與節制，那任何事都是可能成功的。

—— 西奧多・羅斯福（美國第二十六任總統，1858-1919）

With self-discipline most anything is possible.

—Theodore Roosevelt

383

我不知道成功有什麼訣竅，但是我知道失敗的訣竅：那就是試著去討好所有人。

—— 比爾・寇司比（美國喜劇演員、作家、歌手，1937-）

I don't know the key to success, but the key to failure is trying to please everybody.

—Bill Cosby

384

我總是嘗試著將遭遇到的每一場災禍都化為轉機。

—— 約翰‧D‧洛克菲勒
（美國石油大亨、慈善家，1839-1937）

I always tried to turn every disaster into an opportunity.

—John D. Rockefeller, Jr.

385

那些從不敢冒險的人，是喝不到慶祝成功的香檳的。

—— 俄國諺語

He who does not risk will never drink champagne.

—Russian proverb

386

能力是不分性別的。

—— 約翰‧亨利‧紐曼（英國神學家，1801-1890）

Ability is sexless.

—John Henry Newman

387

那些被湮沒在歷史中默默無名的，都是女人。

——維吉尼亞・吳爾芙（英國小說家、散文家，1882-1941）

For most of history, Anonymous was a woman.

——Virginia Woolf

388

幸運女神總是眷顧勇者。

——泰倫提烏斯（羅馬喜劇作家，185-159 B. C.）

Fortune favors the brave.

——Terence

389

我這個人很相信運氣。而我發現當我越努力，
我的運氣就越好。

——湯瑪斯・傑佛遜（美國第三任總統，1743-1826）

I'm a great believer in luck, and I find the harder I work the more I have
of it.

——Thomas Jefferson

390

做事沒有條理的其中一個好處就是，你常常會
有一些意想不到的驚喜與發現。

　　—— 艾倫·亞歷山大·米恩（英國作家，1882－1956）

One of the advantages of being disorderly is that one is constantly
making exciting discoveries. 　　　　　　　　　　—A. A. Milne

391

最勇敢的，就是那些能夠將眼前的一切榮辱都
看得清清楚楚，然後仍能夠毅然去面對的人。

　　　　—— 修昔底德（歷史學家，455－400 B.C.）

The bravest are surely those who have the clearest vision of what is
before them, glory and danger alike, and yet notwithstanding go out to
meet it. 　　　　　　　　　　　　　　　　—Thucydides

392

永遠都不要低頭、永遠都不要放棄並頹然飲泣。嘗試著去找尋別的出路。而如果你只在遭遇困難時才想到要祈禱，那還是別浪費自己和神的時間吧。

—— 薩奇・佩吉（美國大聯盟棒球選手，1906-1982）

Never let your head hang down. Never give up and sit down and grieve. Find another way. And don't pray when it rains if you don't pray when the sun shines.
　　　　　　　　　　　　　　　　　—Satchel Paige

393

你會對所有你沒抓住的射門機會而感到後悔。

—— 韋恩・格雷茨基（加拿大職業冰球選手、教練，1961-）

You'll always miss 100% of the shots you don't take.
　　　　　　　　　　　　　　　　　—Wayne Gretzky

394

一分錢一分貨；那些老想著貪便宜的人最終是會吃大虧的。

—— 約翰・羅斯金（英國藝術評論家，1819-1900）

There is hardly anything in the world that some man can't make a little worse and sell a little cheaper, and the people who consider price only are this man's lawful prey.
　　　　　　　　　　　　　　　　　—John Ruskin

395

當我們嘗試欺騙的時候，我們就編織了可能會束縛自己的羅網。

—— 華爾特・司各特爵士（蘇格蘭小說家，1771 - 1832）

Oh, the tangled webs we weave / When we practice to deceive.
—Sir Walter Scott

396

如果你能夠睿智地學習並運用經驗，那沒有什麼事是浪費時間的。

—— 奧古斯特・羅丹（法國雕刻家，1840 - 1917）

Nothing is a waste of time if you use the experience wisely.
—Auguste Rodin

397

那些在我們身後和在我們眼前的事物，都比不上那些蘊含在我們內心的思想。

—— 拉爾夫・沃爾多・愛默生
（美國哲學家、詩人，1803 - 1882）

What lies behind us and what lies before us are tiny matters compared to what lies within us.　　　　—Ralph Waldo Emerson

398

工作所需的時間會隨著你所擁有的時間而延長：
給自己太多時間，反而會影響效率。

—— 西里爾・諾斯古德・帕金森
（英國作家、社會學家、管理學家，1909-1993）

Work expands to fill the time available for its completion.
—Cyril Northcote Parkinson

399

凡是可能會出錯的事，必定會出錯。

—— 墨菲定律＊

If anything can go wrong, it will.
—Murphy's Law

＊以美國空軍的愛德華・A・墨菲上校為名。他參與了高速載人工
具火箭雪橇的開發計畫，有感於該計畫中錯誤不斷，遂發表此
名言，描述事情總是往最壞處發展。

400

我並沒有失敗；我只是發現了一萬種行不通的
方法而已。

　　　——湯瑪斯・愛迪生（美國發明家，1847-1931）

I have not failed. I've just found 10,000 ways that won't work.

　　　　　　　　　　　　　——Thomas Alva Edison

401

成功之道在於：謹慎地承諾，並且戮力以赴。

——湯瑪斯・彼得斯（奈及利亞解放黑奴領袖、獅子山共和
國建國者之一，1738-1792）

Formula for success: Underpromise and overdeliver.

　　　　　　　　　　　　　——Thomas Peters

402

躲避問題的最好方法就是解決它。

　　　　　　　　　　　　　——佚名

The best way to escape from a problem is to solve it.

　　　　　　　　　　　　　——Anonymous

403

一個有創造力之人的動力，是來自達成自我成就的渴望，而非勝過別人的執念。

—— 艾伊・蘭德（俄裔美國小說家、哲學家，1905–1982）

A creative man is motivated by the desire to achieve, not by the desire to beat others.　　　　　　　　　　　　　—Ayn Rand

404

如果你能夠了解自己從何而來，你就能毫無侷限地走向任何地方。

—— 詹姆斯・鮑德溫（美國作家、評論家，1924–1987）

Know from whence you came. If you know whence you came, there are absolutely no limitations to where you can go.

—James Baldwin

405

再也沒有比成功更為有效的消毒劑了。

—— 丹尼爾・J・布爾斯廷
（美國歷史學家、前美國國會圖書館館長，1914–2004）

There is no disinfectant like success.　　　　—Daniel J. Boorstin

406

一事成功，事事都將成功。

> —— 大仲馬（法國小說家，1802-1870）

Nothing succeeds like success. —Alexander Dumas

407

何物其堅勝過頑石？柔軟勝過弱水？然滴水可以穿石，此誠毅力為然也。

> —— 奧維德（羅馬詩人，43 B. C. -17 A. D.）

What is harder than rock, or softer than water? Yet soft water hollows out hard rock. Persevere. —Ovid

408

昌順能夠教會我們一些事情，但逆境才更是一位偉大的導師。

> —— 威廉·赫茲利特（英國散文作家，1778-1830）

Prosperity is a great teacher; adversity a greater. —William Hazlitt

409

如果我的目光能夠比別人更為長遠，只因我站在巨人的肩膀上。

—— 牛頓（英國數學家、物理學家，1642-1727）

If I have seen further than others, it is by standing upon the shoulders of giants.
　　　　　　　　　　　　　　　　　　　　—Sir Isaac Newton

410

追求勝利與卓越的精神意志，乃是亙古不變的。這些無形的特質要比實際上發生的事情重要得太多了。

—— 文斯・隆巴迪（美國職業足球明星、教練，1913-1970）

The spirit, the will to win, and the will to excel are the things that endure. These qualities are so much more important than the events that occur.　　　　　　　　　　　　　　　　—Vince Lombardi

411

歷史給我們的其中一個教訓就是：謹言慎行。

—— 威爾・杜蘭特（美國歷史學家、散文家，1885-1981）

One of the lessons of history is that nothing is often a good thing to do and always a clever thing to say.　　　　　　　　—Will Durant

412

把事情做好做對，就能夠省下解釋自己為何犯錯的時間。

—— 亨利·沃茲沃思·朗費羅（美國詩人，1807－1882）

It takes less time to do a thing right, than it does to explain why you did it wrong.
　　　　　　　　　　　　　　　　—Henry Wadsworth Longfellow

413

脫韁之馬奔跑的速度再快，也是毫無意義與價值。

—— 尚·考克多
（法國詩人、小說家、劇作家、導演，1889－1963）

The speed of a runaway horse counts for nothing.
　　　　　　　　　　　　　　　　　　—Jean Cocteau

414

一個人在每天都至少要完成一件挑戰自我極限的事。

—— L·羅恩·賀伯特
（美國作家、山達基教創始人，1911－1986）

No one ever gets far unless he accomplishes the impossible at least once a day.
　　　　　　　　　　　　　　　　　　—L. Ron Hubbard

415

所謂完美的境界，並非在於已不能錦上添花，
而是在於不能減損其一分一毫。

—— 安托萬・德・聖修伯里（法國作家，1900-1944）

Perfection is achieved, not when there is nothing left to add, but when
there is nothing left to take away.　　　　—Antoine de Saint-Exupéry

416

如果凡人的脆弱與神的安適無憂能同時並存在
一個人身上，那才稱得上是真正的偉大。

—— 塞內卡
（古羅馬哲學家、政治家、劇作家，4B.C.-65 A.D.）

It is true greatness to have in one the frailty of a man and the security of
a god.　　　　—Lucius Annaeus Seneca

417

所謂成功，端看你從谷底反彈之後能跳得多高。

—— 喬治・巴頓（美國將軍，1885-1945）

Success is how high you bounce when you hit bottom.
　　　　—George Smith Patton, Jr.

418

晴天借傘，雨天收回。這就是銀行的所作所為。

—— 羅伯特・佛洛斯特（美國詩人，1874-1963）

A bank is a place where they lend you an umbrella in fair weather and ask for it back when it begins to rain.　　　　—Robert Frost

419

我們總是在嘗試過失敗的方法之後，找到成功之道。那些從來不犯錯的人，可能也永遠無法有任何新發現。

—— 塞繆爾・史邁爾（蘇格蘭作家，1812-1904）

We often discover what will do, by finding out what will not do; and probably he who never made a mistake never made a discovery.

—Samuel Smiles

420

人生教會我的其中一件事：如果你對一件事感
興趣，你就不再需要去找尋更多新興趣；新的
興趣會接踵而至。當你真心地對一件事感興趣
的時候，它就會引領你走向意想不到的新世界。

—— 愛蓮娜・羅斯福

（前美國第一夫人、外交官，1884-1962）

One thing life taught me: if you are interested, you never have to look
for new interests. They come to you. When you are genuinely interested
in one thing, it will always lead to something else.

—Eleanor Roosevelt

421

若你想要為世界盡一份心力，你必須要先了解
自我，以及了解什麼事物給了你生命的意義。

—— 羅勃特・白朗寧（英國詩人，1812-1889）

To do good thing in the world, first you must know who you are and
what gives meaning to your life. —Robert Browning

422

別想著得到可以一步登天的運氣。無論是友情
或機遇，都是一步一腳印累積起來的。

—— 芭芭拉·布希（前美國第一夫人，1925-）

You just don't luck into things as much as you'd like to think you do.
You build step by step, whether it's friendships or opportunities.

—Barbara Bush

423

無論你認為你做得到還是做不到，你都是對的。

—— 亨利·福特（美國汽車大亨，1863-1947）

Whether you think you can or whether you think you can't, you're
right. —Henry Ford

424

所謂的不順遂，其實代表的是一趟新的冒險。

—— G·K·卻斯特頓（英國作家，1874-1936）

An inconvenience is only an adventure wrongly considered; an adventure
is an inconvenience rightly considered. —G. K. Chesterton

425

睿智之人懂得在今日就準備好明日之事，他也
懂得別將雞蛋都放在同一個籃子裡。

—— 塞萬提斯（西班牙作家，1547-1616）

It is the part of a wise man to keep himself to-day for to-morrow, and
not to venture all his eggs in one basket.

—Miguel de Cervantes

426

想要討好所有人，那是不可能的。在我認真做
事時，我大概會得罪所有人。

—— 喬治·華盛頓（美國第一任總統，1732-1799）

To please everybody is impossible; were I to undertake it, I should
probably please nobody. —George Washington

427

在這八十七年的歲月中，我見證了一連串科技
的革新。但是沒有任何一樣能夠取代個人的品
格和思考的能力。

—— 伯納德·巴魯克（美國金融家、政策顧問，1870-1965）

During my eighty-seven years I have witnessed a whole succession of
technological revolutions. But none of them has done away with the
need for character in the individual or the ability to think.

—Bernard Mannes Baruch

428

多聽少說。

—— 威廉・莎士比亞（英國劇作家，1564－1616）

Listen to many, speak to a few. —William Shakespeare

429

遠離那些總是輕視你的理想與抱負的小人。真正偉大的人會讓你感受到你有朝一日也能夠成就同樣的偉業。

—— 馬克・吐溫（美國作家，1835-1910）

Keep away from people who try to belittle your ambitions. Small people always do that, but the really great make you feel that you too, can become great. —Mark Twain

430

一個能夠馬上執行的好方案，比一個要十分鐘之後才能執行的完美方案要實用得多。

—— 喬治・巴頓（美國將軍，1885-1945）

A good solution applied with vigor now is better than a perfect solution applied ten minutes later. —George Smith Patton, Jr.

431

「英雄」大概是這世上最短命的職業了。

——威爾‧羅傑斯（美國喜劇演員，1879-1935）

Being a hero is about the shortest-lived profession on earth.

—Will Rogers

432

有一天愛麗絲來到了一個路的叉口，看到樹上有一隻面帶微笑的貓。愛麗絲問道：「我該走哪條路呢？」貓回答：「妳想去哪裡？」愛麗絲回答：「我不知道。」貓說：「如果這樣的話，走哪條路都可以。」

——路易斯‧卡羅（英國作家，1832-1898）

One day Alice came to a fork in the road and saw a Cheshire cat in a tree. "Which road do I take?" she asked. "Where do you want to go?" was his response. "I don't know," Alice answered. "Then," said the cat, "it doesn't matter."

—Lewis Carroll

433

如果人長久以來都是被餵食而過活，那他所認識的，就只不過是湯匙的形狀罷了。

—— E·M·佛斯特（英國作家，1879－1970）

Spoon feeding in the long run teaches us nothing but the shape of the spoon.
　　　　　　　　　　　　　　　　　　　—E. M. Forster

434

如果我曾經做出任何有價值的發現，那都要歸功於耐心與專注，而非任何其他的天賦。

—— 牛頓（英國數學家、物理學家，1642－1727）

If I have ever made any valuable discoveries, it has been owing more to patient attention, than to any other talent.　　—Sir Isaac Newton

435

人如果一開始就有既定成見，那必將以懷疑為終點。但是如果能一開始就帶有懷疑的精神，最終必定能得到明確的答案。

—— 法蘭西斯·培根爵士
（英國哲學家、散文作家，1561－1626）

If a man will begin with certainties, he shall end in doubts; but if he will be content to begin with doubts he shall end in certainties.
　　　　　　　　　　　　　　　　　　　—Sir Francis Bacon

436

我不只運用我自己所有的智慧，也借用別人所擁有的智慧。

—— 伍德羅・威爾遜（美國第二十八任總統，1856-1924）

I not only use all the brains that I have, but all that I can borrow.

—Woodrow Wilson

437

人們常說時間會改變一切，但是事實上，有很多事情是你得親自動手去改變的。

—— 安迪・沃荷（美國普普藝術家，1928-1987）

They say that time changes things, but you actually have to change them yourself.

—Andy Warhol

438

人生中一個既弔詭卻又深刻的事實與原則，就是成功之道不在於瞄準你的目標，而是要有超越你原先目標的更遠大志向。

—— 阿諾爾德・約瑟・湯恩比（英國歷史學家，1889-1975）

It is a paradoxical but profoundly true and important principle of life that the most likely way to reach a goal is to be aiming not at that goal itself but at some more ambitious goal beyond it.

—Arnold Joseph Toynbee

439

一個容不得任何修改的計畫，就是個糟糕的計畫。

—— 普布里烏斯·西魯斯 (古羅馬作家，85-43 B.C.)

It is a bad plan that admits of no modification.

—Publilius Syrus

440

與其殷切地盼望一件事，不如著手計畫實行那件事，因為兩者耗費的心力相當。

—— 愛蓮娜·羅斯福
(前美國第一夫人、外交官，1884-1962)

It takes as much energy to wish as it does to plan.

—Eleanor Roosevelt

441

相信自由意志與個人責任的惱人後果就是：你
很難找到一個可以怪罪的人。而當你真的找到
了，你不巧發現那罪人就是你自己。

——P·J·歐魯克（美國政治諷刺作家、記者，1947-）

One of the annoying things about believing in free will and individual
responsibility is the difficulty of finding somebody to blame your
problems on. And when you do find somebody, it's remarkable how
often his picture turns up on your driver's license.　　——P. J. O'Rourke

442

有膽量的人就會是贏家。

——佚名

Who dares, wins.　　　　　　　　　　　　——Anonymous

443

譬如為山，未成一簣，止，吾止也。譬如平地，
雖覆一簣，進，吾往也。

——孔子（中國哲學家，551-479 B. C.）

It does not matter how slowly you go so long as you do not stop.

——Confucius

444

我從老師身上學到的，不比我從書上學到的多。
而我從書上學到的，不比我從我的錯誤中學到
的多。

—— 佚名

I learned much from my teachers, more from my books, and most from
my mistakes. —Anonymous

445

一個睿智的人懂得如何在現有機遇之外，創造
出更多的機會。

—— 法蘭西斯·培根爵士
（英國哲學家、散文作家，1561－1626）

A wise man will make more opportunities than he finds.
—Sir Francis Bacon

446

如果鎚子是你唯一的工具，那你很容易將每件事都當作釘子來處理。

—— 亞伯拉罕・馬斯洛（美國心理學家，1908－1970）

If the only tool you have is a hammer, every problem looks like a nail.

—Abraham Maslow

447

除了掌握機會之外，重要的是學會如何在適當的時候放棄優勢。

—— 班傑明・狄斯雷利（英國前首相、作家，1804－1881）

Next to knowing when to seize an opportunity, the next important thing is to know when to forego an advantage.

—Benjamin Disraeli

448

你當領導我，或者跟隨我，否則就滾開吧！

—— 湯瑪斯・潘恩（英裔美國政治家、思想家，1737－1809）

Lead, follow, or get out of the way.

—Thomas Paine

449

從一個人在賭桌上的舉止，就能看清他的品格。
　　　——威廉·沙洛仁（美國小說家、劇作家，1908-1981）

The manner in which a man chooses to gamble indicates his character or
his lack of it.
　　　　　　　　　　　　　　　　　　　—William Saroyan

450

若你期望在世上昂首前進，
你必得提升自己的價值；
你必須吹響自己的號角、讓世界震驚。
否則的話，相信我，你毫無機會。
　　　　　　　　——威廉·S·吉伯特爵士
　　　　　　（英國劇作家、歌劇作詞家、詩人，1836-1911）

If you wish in this world to advance,
Your merits you're bound to enhance;
You must stir it and stump it,
and blow your own trumpet.
Or trust me, you haven't a chance.
　　　　　　　　　　　　　　　—Sir William S. Gilbert

451

領導意味著解決問題。當有一天你的士兵不再
替你帶來問題時，那就是你的領導終結之日。
他們不是對你喪失信心，就是認為你根本不在
乎。而這兩種情況都表示你是個失敗的領導者。

——科林·鮑爾（前美國國務卿，1937-）

Leadership is solving problems. The day soldiers stop bringing you their
problems is the day you have stopped leading them. They have either
lost confidence that you can help or concluded you do not care. Either
case is a failure of leadership. —Colin Powell

452

你不能總是得到你所渴望的，但是有時你會發
現，你得到的是你所需要的。

——米克·傑格（英國搖滾樂手，1943-）與基思·理查茲
（英國搖滾樂手，1943-）

You can't always get what you want / But if you try sometime you
might find / You get what you need.

—Mick Jagger and Keith Richards

453

成功仰賴努力。

—— 索福克勒斯（希臘悲劇作家，496-405 B.C.）

Success is dependent on effort. —Sophocles

454

庫存可以被管控，員工可不行。他們需要的是領導。

—— H·羅斯·佩羅（美國企業家、美國總統候選人，1930-）

People cannot be managed. Inventories can be managed, but people must be led. —H. Ross Perot

455

如果你相信你能做到，你應該就真能做到；如果你相信你做不到，那你必然會失敗。信念就像是火箭的發射引擎，能夠帶領你脫離平台、飛向宇宙。

—— 丹尼斯·威特利（美國勵志演說家，1933-）

If you believe you can, you probably can. If you believe you won't, you most assuredly won't. Belief is the ignition switch that gets you off the launching pad. —Denis Waitley

456

黑貓白貓，只要能抓老鼠的就是好貓。

—— 鄧小平（中國政治家，1904-1997）

It doesn't matter if a cat is black or white, so long as it catches mice.

—Deng Xiaoping

457

領導的目的，就在於幫助那些表現較差的人做得更好，然後幫助那些做得很好的人更加精進。

—— 吉姆·羅恩
（美國企業家、作家、勵志演說家，1930-2009）

A good objective of leadership is to help those who are doing poorly to do well and to help those who are doing well to do even better.

—Jim Rohn

458

把「不可能」這個想法從你腦中徹底掃除。

—— 塞繆爾·詹森（英國作家，1709-1784）

Clear your mind of can't.

—Samuel Johnson

459

驕傲在敗壞以先；狂心在跌倒之前。

——《聖經》（箴言第十六章第十八節，中文和合本）

Pride goeth before destruction, and haughty spirit before a fall.
——*The Bible*, Proverbs 16:18

460

傾聽每一個人的意見，可是只對極少數人發表
你自己的意見；
接受每一個人的批評，可是保留你自己的判斷。
盡你的財力購置貴重的衣服……
不要向人告貸，也不要借錢給人；
因為債款放了出去，往往不但丟了本錢，而且
還失去了朋友；
向人告貸的結果，容易養成因循懶惰的習慣。＊

——威廉·莎士比亞（英國劇作家，1564-1616）

. . . Give every man thy ear, but few thy voice;
Take each man's censure, but reserve thy judgment.
Costly thy habit as thy purse can buy . . .
Neither a borrower nor a lender be;
For loan oft loses both itself and friend,
And borrowing dulls the edge of husbandry.

——William Shakespeare

＊原文出自《哈姆雷特》（*Hamlet*）第一幕第三景。引自朱生豪的
譯本（人民文學，2015）。

461

沒有誰是能夠完全靠自己來達成人生的成就。
每一位曾幫助過我們、鼓勵過我們的人，都形
塑了我們的品格與思考，也促成了我們的成就。

—— 喬治・馬修・亞當斯（美國專欄作家，1878-1962）

There is no such thing as a "self-made" person. . . . Everyone who has
ever done a kind deed for us, or spoken one word of encouragement to
us, has entered into the make-up of our character and of our thoughts,
as well as our success.　　　　　　　　—George Matthew Adams

462

我們所遭遇的困難，就好像是一位孕育偉大的
母親。這位嚴厲的母親粗暴地晃動著她的孩子，
希望藉此能夠帶給他力量與堅忍。

—— 威廉・庫蘭・布萊恩
（美國詩人、報社編輯，1794-1878）

Difficulty, my brethren, is the nurse of greatness—a harsh nurse, who
roughly rocks her foster-children into strength and athletic proportion.
　　　　　　　　　　　　　　　　　　—William Cullen Bryant

463

若凡事一成不變，世間就不能得見蝴蝶之美了。

—— 佚名

If nothing ever changed, there'd be no butterflies.

—Anonymous

464

所謂進步，最重要的不在於改變，而在於記憶。如果改變太過絕對且容不得更精進的修正，以及當經驗未能留存時，我們就如同野蠻人一般永遠地故步自封了。那些無法記得過去的人，註定將會不斷地重蹈覆轍。

—— 喬治・桑塔亞那（美國哲學家、詩人，1863-1952）

Progress, far from consisting in change, depends on retentiveness. When change is absolute there remains no being to improve and no direction is set for possible improvement: and when experience is not retained, as among savages, infancy is perpetual. Those who cannot remember the past are condemned to repeat it.

—George Santayana

465

那些缺乏想像力的人，就如同失去羽翼的孤鳥。

—— 穆罕默德・阿里（美國拳擊手，1942-2016）

The man who has no imagination has no wings.

—Muhammad Ali

466

我欣賞那些能夠在逆境中微笑、從痛苦中重整
旗鼓、從自省中讓自己更加勇敢的人。當那些
胸無大志的人退縮時，那些意志堅定且以良心
為本的人，將會貫徹自己的原則，直至生命最
後一刻。

—— 湯瑪斯·潘恩（英裔美國政治家、思想家，1737–1809）

I love the man that can smile in trouble, that can gather strength from
distress, and grow brave by reflection. 'Tis the business of little minds to
shrink, but he whose heart is firm, and whose conscience approves his
conduct, will pursue his principles unto death.

—Thomas Paine

467

我嘗試著在對的時間做對的事。這些事可能微
不足道，但常常是決定勝敗的關鍵。

—— 卡里姆·阿布都·賈霸（前美國職業籃球員，1947–）

I try to do the right thing at the right time. They may just be little
things, but usually they make the difference between winning and
losing.

—Kareem Abdul-Jabar

468

偉大事蹟都是由偉大的冒險所造就的。

—— 希羅多德（古希臘歷史學家，484－425 B. C.）

Great deeds are usually wrought at great risks. —Herodotus

469

一個人的昌順與繁榮，關鍵在於他擁抱他所擁有的，而非去追求一切他所渴望的。

—— 喬佛里·F·阿伯特（美國作家，生平不詳）

Prosperity depends more on wanting what you have than having what you want. —Geoffrey F. Abert

470

如果一件事好到讓人覺得不真實，那多半就不是真的。

—— 佚名

If it sounds too good to be true, it is. —Anonymous

471

永遠不要撿那些會讓你失去信用或喪失自尊的便宜。

——亨利・布魯克斯・亞當斯
（美國歷史學家、作家，1838-1918）

Never esteem anything as of advantage to you that will make you break your word or lose your self-respect.

—Henry Brooks Adams

472

如果你沒有經常遭遇到失敗與挫折，那表示你正在做的事並沒什麼創新之處。

——伍迪・艾倫（美國導演、編劇、演員，1935-）

If you're not failing every now and again, it's a sign you're not doing anything very innovative.

—Woody Allen

473

如果你不喜歡某件事，就去改變它吧。如果你無法改變它，就改變自己的態度。唯一你不該做的，就是抱怨。

——馬婭・安傑盧（美國詩人、人權運動者，1928-2014）

If you don't like something change it. If you can't change it, change your attitude. Don't complain.

—Maya Angelou

474

人是由那些平常不斷重複的行為所塑造的。所以卓越不是一個行動，而是一種習慣。

—— 亞里斯多德（希臘哲學家，384-322 B.C.）

We are what we repeatedly do, Excellence is therefore not an act but a habit. 　　　　　　　　　　　　　　　　　—Aristotle

475

千萬別同專家玩牌，也千萬別在媽媽面前下廚。最後，千萬別和那些身上有大麻煩的女人上床。

—— 納爾遜‧亞格林（美國作家，1909-1981）

Never play cards with a man called Doc, never eat at a place called Mom's, and never sleep with a woman whose troubles are worse than your own. 　　　　　　　　　　　　　　　　　—Nelson Algren

476

少即是多，簡潔中看見美感。

—— 路德維希‧密斯凡德羅（德國建築大師，1886-1969）

Less is more. 　　　　　　　　　　　　　—Ludwig Mies van der Rohe

477

萬事起頭難。

—— 湯瑪斯・傅勒（英國傳教士、作家，1608-1661）

All things are difficult before they are easy. —Thomas Fuller

478

面對困難時，堅持並非總是解決的方法。有時候跳過它去進行另一項工作，或許會有意想不到的收穫。我們在面對某些特定的人或事的時候，需要由不同的角度去處理。

—— 馬修・阿諾德（英國詩人、文學批評家，1822-1888）

It is not always by plugging away at a difficulty and sticking at it that one overcomes it; but, rather, often by working on the one next to it. Certain people and certain things require to be approached on an angle.

—Matthew Arnold

479

一番深刻細微的思考，縱然結果是錯的，也能夠留下具有前瞻性的研究，進而可能促進發現具有高度價值的真相。

—— 以撒・艾西莫夫（俄裔美國科幻小說家，1920-1992）

A subtle thought that is in error may yet give rise to fruitful inquiry that can establish truths of great value. —Isaac Asimov

480

倘若你不能掌控金錢，金錢將成為你的主宰。
貪婪之人與其說擁有財富，不如說他是被財富
所奴役。

——法蘭西斯·培根爵士
（英國哲學家、散文作家，1561-1626）

If money be not thy servant, it will be thy master. The covetous man cannot so properly be said to possess wealth, as that may be said to possess him.
——Sir Francis Bacon

481

我從挫折中學到一件事：灰心氣餒不能帶來任
何幫助。抱持忙碌和樂觀的心態，能夠使你恢
復自信。

——露西兒·鮑爾（美國演員，1911-1989）

One of the things I learned the hard way was that it doesn't pay to get discouraged. Keeping busy and making optimism a way of life can restore your faith in yourself.
——Lucille Ball

482

身處在一個組織階層中，我們將一路升遷，最後達到無能的境界。

—— 勞倫斯·J·彼得（美國教育學家、作家，1919－1988）

In a hierarchy every employee tends to rise to his level of incompetence.
　　　　　　　　　　　　　　　　　　—Laurence J. Peter

483

知道如何取得勝利的人並不少，稀少的是那些懂得如何善用勝利的人。

—— 波利比烏斯（古希臘歷史學家，203－120 B. C.）

Those who know how to win are more numerous than those who know how to make proper use of their victories.　　　—Polybius

484

真正的權柄並非藉由力量顯現，而是藉由真理顯現。

—— 奧諾雷·德·巴爾扎克
（法國小說家、劇作家，1799－1850）

Power is not revealed by striking hard or often, but by striking true.
　　　　　　　　　　　　　　　　　　—Honoré de Balzac

485

數以百萬計的人都曾看過蘋果從樹上掉落，但
唯獨牛頓去探究其背後的原因。

—— 伯納德・巴魯克（美國金融家、政策顧問，1870－1965）

Millions saw the apple fall, but Newton was the one who asked why.

—Bernard Baruch

486

在你認為你已經無所不知之後所學到的事物，
才是最為重要的。

—— 約翰・R・伍登（美國大學籃球教練，1910－2010）

It's what you learn after you know it all that's important.

——John R. Wooden

487

隨你怎麼說吧，但是刺激才是驅使人們更加努
力的動力。

—— 尼基塔・赫魯雪夫（前蘇聯總理，1894－1971）

Call it what you will, incentives are what get people to work harder.

—Nikita Khruschev

488

什麼樣的特質造就好的屬下？最重要的特質就是說出事實的意願了。在這個日益複雜的世界，領導者們越來越依靠屬下來取得資訊，無論那是好消息或是壞消息。能勇敢說出事實的屬下和能夠聆聽的領導者，將成為無往不利的組合。

—— 華倫‧G‧貝寧斯

（美國教育學家、社會學家，1925－2014）

What makes a good follower? The single most important characteristic may well be a willingness to tell the truth. In a world of growing complexity leaders are increasingly dependent on their subordinates for good information, whether the leaders want to hear it or not. Followers who tell the truth and leaders who listen to it are an unbeatable combination.　　　　　　　　　　　—Warren G. Bennis

489

財富的重點並不在於擁有，而在於善用。

—— 拿破崙‧波拿巴（法國皇帝、軍事家，1769－1821）

Riches do not consist in the possession of treasures, but in the use made of them.　　　　　　　　　　　—Napoléon Bonaparte

490

性能最棒的電腦就是人。但要生產出大量的人，
我們並不需要高度專業人員就能做到。

—— 華納・馮・布朗（德裔美籍火箭工程師，1912-1977）

The best computer is a man, and it's the only one that can be mass-produced by unskilled labor. —Wernher von Braun

491

直覺是創造力對你無聲的指引。

—— 法蘭克・卡普拉（美國導演，1897-1991）

A hunch is creativity trying to tell you something.
—Frank Capra

492

一個愚人能讓事情擴大、複雜化，甚至於訴諸
暴力。而要消弭這一切，需要真正的天賦與無
比的勇氣。

—— 愛因斯坦（猶太裔美國物理學家，1879-1955）

Any fool can make things bigger, more complex, and more violent. It takes a touch of genius—and a lot of courage—to move in the opposite direction. —Albert Einstein

493

那些對成功感興趣的人，必須要學會將失敗看作是登上高峰的過程中，正面且不可或缺的要素。

—— 喬伊絲·布洛瑟斯（美國心理學家，1929-2013）

The person interested in success has to learn to view failure as a healthy, inevitable part of the process of getting to the top.

—Dr. Joyce Brothers

494

正確的判斷來自於經驗，而經驗則來自於錯誤的判斷。

—— 佚名

Good judgment comes from experience, and experience usually comes from bad judgment.

—Anonymous

495

一個人的志向應該要遠超過他所能掌握的，否則人們何須嚮往天堂？

—— 羅勃特·白朗寧（英國詩人，1812-1889）

Ah, but a man's reach should exceed his grasp—or what's a heaven for?

—Robert Browning

496

建立自信之道在於嘗試去做自己所恐懼的事，
並且記錄下成功的經驗。命運非關機率，而在
於選擇。你不能夠等待命運，你必須親手去掌
握它。

—— 威廉·詹寧斯·布萊恩
（美國政治家、律師，1860-1925）

The way to develop self-confidence is to do the thing you fear and get a
record of successful experiences behind you. Destiny is not a matter of
chance, it is a matter of choice; it is not a thing to be waited for, it is a
thing to be achieved.
　　　　　　　　　　　　　　　　—William Jennings Bryan

497

施捨有害於人，除非這份施捨能讓人更加獨立
自主。

—— 約翰·D·洛克菲勒
（美國石油大亨、慈善家，1839-1937）

Charity is injurious unless it helps the recipient to become independent
of it.
　　　　　　　　　　　　　　　　—John D. Rockefeller, Jr.

498

倘若只憑信念，你能完成的事情並不多，但是
如果沒有信念，你什麼事都做不成。

——塞繆爾·巴特勒（英國詩人、作家，1612-1680）

You can do very little with faith, but you can do nothing without it.
—Samuel Butler

499

跟隨你內心的喜樂，人生的門扉就會在意想不
到的地方開啟。甚至會在其他人所看不到的地
方獨自為你開啟。

——喬瑟夫·坎伯（美國神話學家、作家，1904-1987）

When you follow your bliss . . . doors will open where you would not
have thought there would be doors; and where there wouldn't be a door
for anyone else.
—Joseph Campbell

500

許多人永遠都無法了解，你越是試著要躲避苦難，你就會越痛苦。因為一些枝微末節的事物也會因你的恐懼而變得巨大，進而開始折磨你。

—— 湯瑪斯・莫頓（美國天主教神學家、作家，1915－1968）

The truth that many people never understand, until it is too late, is that the more you try to avoid suffering the more you suffer because smaller and more insignificant things begin to torture you in proportion to your fear of being hurt.

—Thomas Merton

501

你可以藉由友善的話語取得一些進展，而如果同時你手上有一把槍的話，則效果更加顯著。

—— 艾爾・卡彭（美國黑手黨大佬，1899－1947）

You can get a lot farther with a kind word and a gun than a kind word alone.

—Al Capone

502

沒有目標的人就好像一艘沒有舵的船：一個無足輕重的浪人、甚至不能算得上是個人。一定要為自己的生活設定目標並努力去達成。遵照神的旨意，將你的心力都投入到工作中吧！

—— 湯瑪斯·卡萊爾（英國歷史學家，1795-1881）

The man without a purpose is like a ship without a rudder—a waif, a nothing, a no man. Have a purpose in life and having it, throw such strength of mind and muscle into your work as God has given you.

—Thomas Carlyle

503

從該開始的地方開始 ...... 在該結束的地方結束。

—— 路易斯·卡羅（英國作家，1832-1898）

"Begin at the beginning…and go on till you come to the end: then stop."

—Lewis Carroll

504

所有拿薪水的工作，都會消耗人的心靈，降低人的心智。

—— 亞里斯多德（希臘哲學家，384-322 B.C.）

All paid jobs absorb and degrade the mind.

—Aristotle

505

我自己是個樂觀主義者。如果不保持樂觀的話，
我看不出來對人生有何好處。

—— 溫斯頓・邱吉爾（前英國首相，1874-1965）

For myself I am an optimist—it does not seem to be much use being
anything else.　　　　　　　　　　　　—Sir Winston Churchill

506

世界上沒有任何特質能夠取代堅忍。天賦？在
世上多的是擁有天賦卻無法成功的人。才華？
懷才不遇的例子也是多不勝數。教育？社會上
也是隨處可見高學歷的無業遊民。因為堅忍和
決心才是能達成一切的特質。

—— 卡爾文・柯立芝（美國第三十任總統，1872-1933）

Nothing in the world can take the place of persistence. Talent will not;
nothing is more common than unsuccessful men with talent. Genius
will not; unrewarded genius is almost a proverb. Education will not;
the world is full of educated derelicts. Persistence and determination are
omnipotent.　　　　　　　　　　　　　　　—Calvin Coolidge

507

鐵無用則鏽蝕，水若停滯則不再純淨，且會在
天冷時凍結。而人若是無為，就會弱化心靈的
活力。

—— 李奧納多‧達文西
（義大利藝術家、發明家，1492-1519）

Iron rusts from disuse; stagnant water loses it purity and in cold weather
becomes frozen; even so does inaction sap the vigor of the mind.

—Leonardo da Vinci

508

相信那些正在尋找真理的人；而對那些聲稱已
經找到的人，要心存懷疑。

—— 安德烈‧紀德（法國作家，1869-1951）

Believe those who are seeking the truth; doubt those who find it.

—André Gide

509

其實冒險一試才是唯一安全的做法。打安全牌
有時是死路一條。冒險乃是偉大事業的本質。
而謹慎與大膽之間的界線，只能由你自己來定
義，因為除了你之外沒有人知道你真正的目標。

—— 麥克·尼可斯（德裔美籍導演，1931-2014）

The only safe thing is to take a chance. Play safe and you are
dead. Taking risks is the essence of good work, and the difference
between safe and bold can only be defined by yourself since no one else
knows for what you are hoping when you embark on anything.

—Mike Nichols

510

有時候你必須扮演別人很長一段時間，才能夠
真正地做回自己。

—— 邁爾斯·戴維斯三世（美國爵士樂音樂家，1926-1991）

Sometimes you have to play for a long time to be able to play like
yourself.　　　　　　　　　　　　　　　　—Miles Davis, Jr.

511

在深夜裡對一道難題百思不解，但在第二天早晨靈光乍現而解，是一個很常見的經驗。

—— 約翰・史坦貝克（美國小說家，1902-1968）

It is a common experience that a problem difficult at night is resolved in the morning after a committee of sleep has worked on it.

—John Steinbeck

512

小小的機遇常常是偉大事業的開端。

—— 狄摩西尼（古希臘政治家、演說家，384-322 B.C.）

Small opportunities are often the beginning of great enterprises.

—Demosthenes

513

如果你都沒犯過任何錯誤，表示你還不夠努力。

—— 文斯・隆巴迪（美國職業足球明星、教練，1913-1970）

If you're not making mistakes, you're not trying hard enough.

—Vince Lombardi

514

失敗是具有啟發性的。一個真正能夠思考的人，
從他的失敗能學到的，不比從他的成功學到的
少。

—— 約翰・杜威（美國哲學家、教育家，1859-1952）

Failure is instructive. The person who really thinks learns quite as much
from his failures as from his successes. —John Dewey

515

在你妥善規劃之後，好運氣自然會跟著來。

—— 布蘭赫・瑞奇（前美國職棒大聯盟執行長，1881-1965）

Luck is the residue of design. —Branch Rickey

516

諦語不瞋恚，分施與乞者；以如是三事，能生
於諸天。

—— 佛教《法句譬喻經》

Speak the truth, do not yield to anger; give, if thou art asked for little;
by these three steps thou wilt go near the gods.
—*The Dhammapada*

517

沒有任何事物是憑空出現的。

—— 第歐根尼·拉爾修
（古羅馬傳記作家，活躍於西元三世紀）

Nothing can be produced out of nothing.　　　　—Diogenes Läertius

518

在你排除了一切不可能的因素之後，無論剩下
的可能性有多麼低，就必需是事情的真相。

—— 亞瑟·柯南·道爾爵士（英國作家，1859-1930）

When you have eliminated the impossible, that which remains, however
improbable, must be the truth.　　　　—Sir Arthur Conan Doyle

519

你不能以你想做但尚未做到的事來建立名聲。

—— 亨利·福特（美國汽車大亨，1863-1947）

You can't build a reputation on what you're going to do.

—Henry Ford

520

最卓越的航海家，懂得如何將狂風巨浪都收為
己用。

—— 愛德華・吉朋（英國歷史學家，1737–1794）

The winds and the waves are always on the side of the ablest navigators.

—Edward Gibbon

521

歲入二十鎊，歲出九鎊六，平安喜樂。歲入
二十鎊，歲出二十鎊六，嗚呼哀哉。

—— 查爾斯・狄更斯（英國小說家，1812–1870）

Annual income twenty pounds, annual expenditure nineteen pounds
and six, result happiness. Annual income twenty pounds, annual
expenditure twenty pounds ought and six, result misery.

—Charles Dickens

522

別將你的狗對你的愛慕，當作是自己出類拔萃
的證明。

—— 安・蘭德斯（當代美國專欄作家筆名，生平不詳）

Don't accept your dog's admiration as conclusive evidence that you are
wonderful.

—Ann Landers

523

倘若沒有熱情，就無法成就任何偉大的事。

——拉爾夫・沃爾多・愛默生
（美國哲學家、詩人，1803－1882）

Nothing great was ever achieved without enthusiasm.

—Ralph Waldo Emerson

524

這個世界上充滿了心甘情願的人；有些人心甘情願地努力，有些人則是心甘情願地袖手旁觀。

——羅伯特・佛洛斯特（美國詩人，1874－1963）

The world is full of willing people; some willing to work, the rest willing to let them.

—Robert Frost

525

我尊敬那些清楚了解自己渴望的人。這世上許多的不幸，都是來自於人們無法認知自己的目標。他們想要建造一座高塔，所花費的努力卻連一座茅屋的地基都打不了。

——歌德（德國戲劇家、詩人，1749-1832）

I respect the man who knows distinctly what he wishes. The greater part of all mischief in the world arises from the fact that men do not sufficiently understand their own aims. They have undertaken to build a tower, and spend no more labor on the foundation than would be necessary to erect a hut. —Johann Wolfgang von Goethe

526

倘若你狎玩你內心中的野獸，你難免會化身為真正的野獸。倘若你心懷詐欺，就難免會背離真理。倘若你心懷殘酷的念頭，則難免會喪失情感。倘若你希望你的方寸之地是一塊淨土，就不能容許野草的叢生。

——道格·哈瑪紹
（瑞典外交家、前聯合國秘書長，1905-1961）

You cannot play with the animal in you without becoming wholly animal, play with falsehood without forfeiting your right to truth, play with cruelty without losing your sensitivity of mind. He who wants to keep his garden tidy doesn't reserve a plot for weeds. —Dag Hammarskjöld

527

在藝術方面，比起一件技巧純熟但格局狹隘的
作品，我更為欣賞一件技巧粗糙但意圖宏大的
作品。換句話說，我認為崇高的理念要比精妙
的表現手法重要得多。

—— 湯瑪士·哈代（英國小說家、詩人，1840-1928）

My weakness has always been to prefer the large intention of an
unskillful artist to the trivial intention of an accomplished one: in other
words, I am more interested in the high ideas of a feeble executant than
in the high execution of a feeble thinker. —Thomas Hardy

528

我的品味很簡單。我對於最棒的事物總是感到
滿意。

—— 奧斯卡·王爾德（愛爾蘭文學家，1854-1900）

I have the simplest tastes. I am always satisfied with the best.

—Oscar Wilde

529

我們遠比我們所以為的要睿智得多。

—— 拉爾夫·沃爾多·愛默生
（美國哲學家、詩人，1803-1882）

We are wiser than we know. —Ralph Waldo Emerson

530

幸福就好像一隻飛舞的蝴蝶，當你想要追求時，
她總是翩翩逃離你的掌握。但是當你安坐不動，
她就可能會停駐在你身上。

—— 納撒尼爾‧霍桑（美國作家，1804-1864）

Happiness is as a butterfly which, when pursued, is always beyond our grasp, but which if you will sit down quietly, may alight upon you.

—Nathaniel Hawthorne

531

人生中將有一陣浪潮，
倘若能夠順勢而前，將功成名就。
若是錯過，則人生的旅程
將深陷於黑影和不幸中。

—— 威廉‧莎士比亞（英國劇作家，1564-1616）

There is a tide in the affairs of men,
Which taken at the flood, leads on to fortune;
Omitted, all the voyage of their life
Is bound in shallows and in miseries.

—William Shakespeare

532

我發現世上最重要的事，不是我們所處在的位置，而是我們前進的方向。我們必須啟航，有時順應潮流，有時必須逆流而上。勇往直前，而非徘徊或停滯不前。

—— 小奧利弗·溫德爾·霍姆斯
（美國法學家、最高法院大法官，1841-1935）

I find the great thing in this world is not so much where we stand, as in what direction we are moving—we must sail sometimes with the wind and sometimes against it—but we must sail, and not drift, nor lie at anchor. 　　　　　　　　　　　　　—Oliver Wendell Holmes, Jr.

533

我有過美夢也有過惡夢，但是我已經藉由美好的夢想克服了那些我所恐懼的事物。

—— 喬納斯·索爾克（美國醫學家、病毒學家，1914-1995）

I have had dreams and I have had nightmares, but I have conquered my nightmares because of my dreams. 　　　　　　　　—Jonas Salk

534

許多瑣碎的細節造就完美，但是完美本身絕非瑣碎。

—— 米開朗基羅（義大利文藝復興時期藝術家，1475-1564）

Trifles make perfection, and perfection is no trifle.

—Michelangelo

535

不光明磊落的成功就好像沒有調味好的菜餚，可以讓你吃個粗飽，但是卻淡而無味。

—— 喬·帕特諾（美國賓州大學美式足球隊教練，1926-2012）

Success without honor is an unseasoned dish; it will satisfy your hunger, but it won't taste good.

—Joe Paterno

536

經驗並非你所遭遇到的事情，而是你應對那些事情的方式與態度。

—— 阿道斯·赫胥黎（英國小說家，1894-1963）

Experience is not what happens to you, it is what you do with what happens to you.

—Aldous Huxley

537

沒有任何事物是穩固如磐石的。所有事物都是
建立在細沙之上，搖搖欲墜。但是我們必須將
細沙視作磐石一般地建立自己。

—— 豪爾赫·路易斯·波赫士
（阿根廷作家、詩人、翻譯家，1899－1986）

Nothing is built on stone; all is built on sand, but we must build as if the
sand were stone. —Jorge Luis Borges

538

一個人必須要有承認自己錯誤的氣量、從錯誤
中學習的智慧，以及改正錯誤的勇氣與堅強。

—— 約翰·C·馬克斯韋爾（美國作家，1947－）

A man must be big enough to admit his mistakes, smart enough to
profit from them, and strong enough to correct them.
—John C. Maxwell

539

若在做任何事之前需要克服所有的反對聲音，
那你永遠都不可能有進展。

—— 塞繆爾·詹森（英國作家，1709－1784）

Nothing will ever be attempted if all possible objections must first be
overcome. —Samuel Johnson

540

這世界上只有一種成功，那就是以你自己的方式生活。

—— 克里斯多福‧達林頓‧莫里
（美國作家、編輯，1890-1957）

There is only one success—to be able to spend your life in your own way.
—Christopher Darlington Morley

541

這世上最可悲的人，就是那些只看得見眼前的事物，但卻看不到未來願景的人。

—— 海倫‧凱勒（美國作家、社會運動家、講師，1880-1968）

The most pathetic person in the world is someone who has sight, but has no vision.
—Helen Keller

542

沒有求知的欲望，就永遠不可能學得新的事物。

—— 傑里‧加西亞（美國歌手、作詞家，1942-1995）

You ain't gonna learn what you don't wanna know.
—Jerry Garcia

543

如果你問我，是否有一個對全人類來說最有用
的建議，我會這樣告訴你：將困難想像成生命
中不可或缺的一部份吧，正視你的困難，然後
對著它說：我將會超越你；你無法擊敗我。

—— 安·蘭德斯（當代美國專欄作家筆名，生平不詳）

If I were asked to give what I consider the single most useful bit of
advice for all humanity, it would be this: Expect trouble as an inevitable
part of life. . . . Look it squarely in the eye, and say, I will be bigger than
you. You cannot defeat me.　　　　　　　　　　　—Ann Landers

544

如果人們能夠以更開闊的心胸去看待生活中所
發生的事情，他們將會時常發現：那些他們無
法得到的事物，其實並非是他們真正渴望的。

—— 安德烈·莫洛亞（法國傳記作家，1885－1967）

If men could regard the events of their own lives with more open minds,
they would frequently discover that they did not really desire the things
they failed to obtain.　　　　　　　　　　　　　—André Maurois

545

對於一個人辛勤努力的最高獎賞，並非他靠著努力所得到的事物，而是藉由努力，他已成為了一個更好的人。

——約翰‧羅斯金（英國藝術評論家，1819-1900）

The highest reward for a man's toil is not what he gets for it but what he becomes by it.　　　　　　　　　　　—John Ruskin

546

訓練並不能夠造就完美。精確到完美程度的練習才能。

——文斯‧隆巴迪（美國職業足球明星、教練，1913-1970）

Practice doesn't make perfect. Perfect practice makes perfect.
　　　　　　　　　　　　　　　　　—Vince Lombardi

547

做一個成功的人，和做一個失敗的人，都有著同樣的壓力。

——艾密利歐‧詹姆斯‧圖吉洛
（美國業餘哲學家，生平不詳）

It takes as much stress to be a success as it does to be a failure.
　　　　　　　　　　　　　　　　—Emilio James Trujillo

548

當你孤身一人與全世界對抗時，還是趕緊投降並站在世界的那一邊吧。

——法蘭茲‧卡夫卡（波希米亞德語小說家，1883-1924）

In the fight between you and the world, back the world.

——Franz Kafka

549

對於身而為人會遭遇到的問題，總會有個看似簡單的解決方法。它八面玲瓏、看似頗有道理，但事實上卻是大錯特錯的。

——H‧L‧孟肯（美國編輯、評論家，1880-1956）

There is always an easy solution to every human problem—neat, plausible, and wrong.

——H. L. Mencken

550

想像力時常將我們引導至虛無的世界。但是如果沒有了想像力，我們哪兒都去不了。

——卡爾‧薩根（美國天文學家、科普作家，1934-1996）

Imagination will often carry us to worlds that never were. But without it we go nowhere.

——Carl Sagan

551

所謂懦夫，就是在危險來臨前驚懼，危險過程
中畏縮，危險過後卻自稱勇者的人。

—— 讓·保羅（德國作家，1763－1825）

A timid person is frightened before a danger, a coward during the time,
and a courageous person afterward.

—Jean Paul Friedrich Richter

552

若你想把壞習慣請出家門，你不能直接把它丟
出窗外，而是要先慢慢地勸服它走下一階一階
的樓梯。

—— 馬克·吐溫（美國作家，1835－1910）

A habit cannot be tossed out the window; it must be coaxed down the
stairs a step at a time.

—Mark Twain

553

偶然發生的意外就好像一把利刃，它能夠割傷你，也能夠為你所用。端看你握的是劍柄還是刀刃。

——詹姆斯・羅素・羅威爾
（美國詩人、外交官，1819-1891）

Mishaps are like knives, that either serve us or cut us, as we grasp them by the blade or the handle.
——James Russell Lowell

554

世上最強大的兩位勇士，就是耐心與時間。

——列夫・托爾斯泰（俄國小說家、哲學家，1828-1910）

The two most powerful warriors are patience and time.
——Leo Tolstoy

555

生命最偉大的榮耀，不在於永不失敗，而在於失敗之後的奮起。

——納爾遜・曼德拉
（南非反種族隔離革命家、政治家、前南非總統，1918-2013）

The greatest glory in living lies not in never falling, but in rising every time we fall.
——Nelson Mandela

556

如果你太過謹慎，你就會太過專注於保持謹慎，
而不小心被什麼給絆了一跤。

—— 葛楚·史坦（美國作家、詩人，1874–1946）

Everybody knows if you are too careful you are so occupied in being
careful that you are sure to stumble over something.
—Gertrude Stein

557

所謂專業人士，就是能夠將自己未必喜歡的事
情做到最好。

—— 亞力斯塔爾·庫克
（英裔美籍媒體人、主播，1908–2004）

A professional is a man who can do his best at a time when he doesn't
particularly feel like it.　　　　　—Alistair Cooke

558

當辛苦開始轉變成痛苦的時候，還能夠堅持下
去的人，才會得到最後的勝利。

—— 羅傑·班尼斯特（英國長跑運動員，1929–）

The man who can drive himself further once the effort gets painful is the
man who will win.　　　　　—Roger Bannister

559

你應該相信，藉由你的情感和行動，你是正在參與冥冥中的偉大事業。你越培養這份信仰，現實與世界就越會成為你的助力。

——萊納·瑪利亞·里爾克（德國詩人，1875-1926）

Do continue to believe that with your feeling and your work you are taking part in the greatest; the more strongly you cultivate this belief, the more will reality and the world go forth from it.

—Rainer Maria Rilke

560

在當下盡你最大的努力，因為這將延續到你未來的表現。

——歐普拉·溫芙蕾
（美國脫口秀主持人、製作人、慈善家，1954-）

Doing the best at this moment puts you in the best place for the next moment.

—Oprah Winfrey

561

沒有任何職業是粗鄙的，有的只是粗鄙的態度。

——威廉·班尼特（美國政治家、前教育部長，1943-）

There are no menial jobs, only menial attitudes.

—William John Bennet

562

錯誤乃是通往新發現之門。

—— 詹姆斯·喬伊斯（愛爾蘭小說家，1882-1941）

Mistakes are the portals for discovery.　　　　　　—James Joyce

563

如果一個學徒從未被要求去做他做不到的事，
那麼他會連能力之內的事都無法做好。

—— 約翰·史都華·彌爾
（英國哲學家、政治經濟學家，1806-1873）

The pupil who is never required to do what he cannot do, never does
what he can do.　　　　　　　　　　　　—John Stuart Mill

564

上帝向來無需
人類的功績或其才能；
那些能順從地穿戴枷鎖者
才是最能侍奉上帝之人。
而那些遵照祂的旨意
奔波於陸地與海上，或靜靜駐足的守望者
也同樣使上帝愉悅。

———約翰·米爾頓（英國詩人，1608-1674）

. . . God doth not need
Either man's work or his own gifts; who best
Bear his mild yoke, they serve him best; his State
is Kingly. Thousands at his bidding speed
And post o'er Land and Ocean without rest:
They also serve who only stand and wait.　　　　—John Milton

565

永遠別告訴手下的士兵如何做事。告訴他們你
希望他們達成的目標，他們的卓越就會讓你感
到驚訝。

———喬治·巴頓（美國將軍，1885-1945）

Never tell people how to do things. Tell them what you want them to
achieve, and they will surprise you with their ingenuity.

—George Smith Patton, Jr.

566

失敗的人有兩種：一種是只思考而無行動，另一種則是想都不想就莽撞行動。

—— 勞倫斯・J・彼得（美國教育學家、作家，1919-1988）

There are two kinds of failures: those who thought and never did, and those who did and never thought.
　　　　　　　　　　　　　　　　　　　　—Laurence J. Peter

567

當你的目光沒有專注在目標上時，所謂的障礙就會順勢出現。

—— 亨利・福特（美國汽車大亨，1863-1947）

Obstacles are those frightful things you see when you take your eyes off your goal.
　　　　　　　　　　　　　　　　　　　　—Henry Ford

568

問題與困難不過就是穿著工作服的機會罷了。

—— 亨利・J・凱薩（美國企業家，1882-1967）

Problems are only opportunities in work clothes.
　　　　　　　　　　　　　　　　　　　　—Henry J. Kaiser

569

善用你所有的才能：倘若只有歌喉最好的鳥兒才能歌唱的話，那林子裡將會寂靜一片。

—— 亨利·范戴克（美國長老教會傳教士，1852-1933）

Use what talents you possess: the woods would be very silent if no birds sang there except those that sang best.　　　　—Henry Van Dyke

570

那些埋首於工作而從未考慮成功與否的人，成功反而會悄然地降臨到他們身上。

—— 亨利·大衛·梭羅
（美國作家、自然主義者，1817-1862）

Success usually comes to those who are too busy to be looking for it.
　　　　—Henry David Thoreau

571

我寧願為一個終將勝利的抱負嘗盡失敗的痛苦，也不願在一個終將失敗的抱負中享受暫時的勝利。

—— 伍德羅·威爾遜（美國第二十八任總統，1856-1924）

I would rather fail in a cause that will ultimately triumph than to triumph in cause that will ultimately fail.

　　　　—Woodrow Wilson

572

在沒有必要的情況下，切莫增加那些需要額外解釋的因素。*

—— 奧坎的威廉
（英國邏輯學家、聖方濟各會修士，1285-1349）

One should not increase, beyond what is necessary, the number of entities required to explain anything.　　　—William of Occam

573

當我在處理一個問題時，我並沒有任何與美感相關的想法。但是當我解決了問題之後，如果我發現我的解法毫無美感，那我無疑是做錯了。

—— R‧巴克敏斯特‧富勒
（美國建築師、工程師，1895-1983）

When I am working on a problem, I never think about beauty . . . but when I have finished, if the solution is not beautiful, I know it is wrong.
　　　—R. Buckminster Fuller

---

* 此為著名的「簡約法則」（lex parsimoniae），又稱為「奧坎剃刀」（Occam's razor）。

574

只有開放的心胸是不夠的，敞開的心胸就像張口欲言的嘴巴一樣，最終都是要在堅實的真理面前乖乖閉上。

——G·K·卻斯特頓（英國作家，1874-1936）

Merely having an open mind is nothing; the object of opening the mind, as of opening the mouth, is to shut it again on something solid.

——G. K. Chesterton

575

願上帝賜福於那些無話可說，因此不會向我們囉唆地解釋一些顯而易見事實的人。

—— 喬治·艾略特（英國小說家，1819-1880）

Blessed is the man who, having nothing to say, abstains from giving us wordy evidence of the fact.

——George Eliot

576

好奇心賦予人們豐富的論述，以及對於各種生命形式愉悅的體會與認同。

——亞力斯塔爾·庫克
（英裔美籍媒體人、主播，1908-2004）

Curiosity . . . endows the people who have it with a generosity in argument and a serenity in cheerful willingness to let life take the form it will.
——Alistair Cooke

577

僅有思想並無法長久。思想必須要靠行動來成就。

——阿爾弗雷德·諾斯·懷海德
（英國數學家、哲學家，1861-1947）

Ideas won't keep; something must be done about them.
——Alfred North Whitehead

578

當人們不斷地說：「你做不來的！」，你就更會感到一股想要嘗試的渴望。

—— 瑪格麗特‧蔡斯‧史密斯
（美國眾議院議員，1897-1995）

When people keep telling you that you can't do a thing, you kind of like to try it.
—— Margaret Chase Smith

579

別在你需要骨氣的時候寄望運氣。

—— 克萊曼婷‧帕德福（美國烹飪作家，1898-1967）

Never grow a wishbone where your backbone ought to be.
—— Clementine Paddleford

580

沒有人能夠使你感到卑微，除非你自己同意。

—— 愛蓮娜‧羅斯福
（前美國第一夫人、外交官，1884-1962）

Nobody can make you feel inferior without your consent.
—— Eleanor Roosevelt

581

善意的話語可以輕易說出，其造成的迴響卻是
恆久遠。

—— 德蕾莎修女
（阿爾巴尼亞裔印度修女、諾貝爾和平獎得主，1910–1997）

Kind words are short and easy to speak, but their echoes are truly
endless.
—Mother Teresa

582

致力於你的夢想吧！那些嘗試去成就偉大事業
但未竟全功的人，絕非是失敗者。因為他總是
能夠確認一件事，那就是他已經成功地打贏了
人生中的重要戰役：他擊敗了嘗試未知事物的
恐懼。

—— 羅伯特·H·舒樂
（美國牧師、電視傳教士，1926–2015）

Commit yourself to a dream. . . Nobody who tries to do something
great but fails is a total failure. Why? Because he can always rest assured
that he succeeded in life's most important battle—he defeated the fear
of trying.
—Robert H. Schuller

583

你也許會為失敗而感到氣餒，但你能夠從失敗中學習。所以勇往直前，切莫害怕犯錯。因為你必須記住，從長遠來看，在錯誤中你將找到成功。

——托馬斯·華生爵士（美國企業家，1874-1956）

You can be discouraged by failure—or you can learn from it. So go ahead and make mistakes. Make all you can. Because, remember that's where you'll find success. On the far side.　　　—Thomas Watson, Sr.

584

我總是努力去做那些我能力範圍之外的事，因為我將學會如何去克服它們。

——巴勃羅·畢卡索（西班牙藝術家，1881-1973）

I am always doing that which I can not do, in order that I may learn how to do it.　　　—Pablo Picasso

585

在你清醒時候，試著去做那些你喝醉時吹噓能
做到的事吧！那會讓你學到寶貴的一課，那就
是應該適時地閉上自己的嘴巴。

—— 厄尼斯特·海明威（美國作家，1899－1961）

Always do sober what you said you'd do drunk. That will teach you to
keep your mouth shut.
　　　　　　　　　　　　　　　　　　—Ernest Hemingway

586

這世上最難以掌握、最危險、最難確保其成功
的事，就是引領一個全新的秩序。

—— 尼可洛·馬基維利
（義大利文藝復興政治家、作家，1469－1527）

There is nothing more difficult to take in hand, more perilous to
conduct, or more uncertain in its success, than to take the lead in the
introduction of a new order to things.　　　—Niccolò Machiavelli

587

一顆鑽石，是一堆碳粒子各司其職的成果。

—— 邁爾康・富比士
（美國企業家、雜誌發行人，1919－1990）

Diamonds are nothing more than chunks of coal that stuck to their jobs.
—Malcolm Forbes

588

心懷大志之人，能夠屈身潛行，也能夠奮然雄起。

—— 埃德蒙・伯克
（英國政治家、哲學家、作家，1729－1797）

Ambition can creep as well as soar.　　　　　—Edmund Burke

589

那些用大理石或黃銅所雕塑成的事物，終將在
時間的流逝中灰飛煙滅。人們所興建的廟堂，
也同樣會歸於塵土。唯有心性上的修養，是時
間所無法磨滅的，它將永恆地閃耀下去。

—— 丹尼爾・韋伯斯特
（美國政治家、前國務卿，1782－1852）

If we work upon marble, it will perish; if we work upon brass, time will
efface it; if we rear temples, they will crumble into dust; but if we work
upon immortal minds and instill into them just principles, we are then
engraving that upon tablets which no time will efface, but will brighten
and brighten to all eternity. —Daniel Webster

590

太上，不知有之；其次，親而譽之；
其次，畏之；其次，侮之。
信不足焉，有不信焉。悠兮其貴言。
功成，事遂，百姓皆謂：「我自然。」

—— 老子（中國哲學家，約西元前七世紀－531 B.C.）

The best leaders of all are ones the people do not know exist. They turn
to each other and say we did it ourselves. —Lao-Tzu

591

他們能真的做到，是因為他們相信他們能做到。

—— 維吉爾（古羅馬詩人，70-19 B.C.）

They can do all because they think they can. —Virgil

592

一張全白的紙頁或帆布，蘊含著何等的可能性啊！

—— 史蒂芬‧桑坦（美國作曲家，1930-）

White. A blank page or canvas. So many possibilities.
—Stephen Sondheim

593

我們都應該為犯點無關緊要的小錯感到驕傲，因為這讓我們覺得，至少沒犯什麼無可挽救的大錯。

—— 安迪‧魯尼（美國傳媒工作者，1919-2011）

We're all proud of making little mistakes. It gives us the feeling we don't make any big ones. —Andy Rooney

594

人類的特色就在於，他們能藉由互相合作，成就更多事，而非互相對抗。

—— 艾倫·佛洛姆（美國心理學家、作家，1916-2003）

People have been known to achieve more as a result of working with others than against them. ——Dr. Allan Fromme

595

世間有四種事物是你永遠無法收回的：說出口的話語、射出去的箭矢、過去，以及那些錯過的機會。

—— 阿拉伯諺語

Four things come not back: the spoken word, the spent arrow, the past, the neglected opportunity. ——Arabic proverb

596

世界上的任何地方都是可以徒步到達的，只要你有時間的話。

—— 史蒂文·萊特（美國喜劇演員，1955-）

Anywhere is walking distance, if you've got the time. ——Steven Wright

597

一個丑角的成功與否，在於聽眾的耳朵，而非他自己的如簧之舌。

——威廉・莎士比亞（英國劇作家，1564-1616）

A jest's prosperity lies in the ear of him that hears it, never in the tongue of him that makes it.   —William Shakespeare

598

相信你自己：你所掌握的知識，遠比你所認為的多。

——班傑明・斯波克（美國兒科醫生、教育家，1903-1998）

Trust yourself. You know more than you think you do.

    —Benjamin Spock

599

我寧願失敗，也要躋身偉大人物的行列。

——約翰・濟慈（英國詩人，1795-1821）

I would sooner fail than not be among the greatest.

    —John Keats

600

任何你所錯過的事物，都會讓你在別的地方有所收穫。

——拉爾夫·沃爾多·愛默生
（美國哲學家、詩人，1803－1882）

For everything you have missed, you have gained something else.
—Ralph Waldo Emerson

601

如果你沒有對手上的工作盡心盡力，你就像是一個只看見船隻開始進水，就準備棄船逃生的人。眾人齊心協力將船划到岸邊不是一件簡單的事，更別說有人早就放棄職守、穿上救生衣了。

——盧·霍茲（美國大學美式足球隊教練，1937－）

If you don't make a total commitment to whatever you're doing, then you start looking to bail out the first time the boat starts leaking. It's tough enough getting that boat to shore with everybody rowing, let alone when a guy stands up and starts putting his jacket on.
—Lou Holtz

602

向滿天繁星伸出雙手：也許你仍無法企及它們，
但是你的雙手將不會沾滿塵泥。

—— 李奧‧貝納（美國廣告企業執行長，1891－1971）

When you reach for the stars, you may not quite get them, but you
won't come up with a handful of mud either. —Leo Burnett

603

當意志戰勝恐懼、當激情與理智相輔相成、當
責任感強大到足以挑戰命運、當榮譽不與死亡
妥協：英雄就此誕生。

—— 羅伯特‧英格索爾
（美國律師、政治家、演說家，1833－1899）

When the will defies fear, when the heart applauds the brain, when duty
throws the gauntlet down to fate, when honor scorns to compromise
with death—this is heroism. —Robert Ingersoll

604

讓恐懼給予你建議，但別讓它束縛了你。

—— 安東尼‧羅賓斯（美國企業家、慈善家、作家，1960－）

Let fear be a counselor and not a jailer. —Anthony Robbins

605

嫉妒由許多成分所組成，其中甚至混雜著人們對正義的渴望。我們對於那些不應得的好運總是感到氣憤。

—— 威廉‧赫茲利特（英國散文作家，1778-1830）

Envy, among other ingredients, has a mixture of love of justice in it. We are more angry at undeserved than at deserved good fortune.

—William Hazlitt

606

萬物也許會亙古不變，但我們的想法終究會改變。

—— 馬塞爾‧普魯斯特（法國作家，1871-1922）

Things don't change, but by and by our wishes change.

—Marcel Proust

607

一旦你決定要完成某件事，儘管有著疲勞與厭惡感，還是用盡一切心力去完成吧！成就一件困難的事，所得到自信是無與倫比的。

—— 阿諾德‧貝內特（英國小說家，1867-1931）

Having once decided to achieve a certain task, achieve it at all cost of tedium and distaste. The gain in self-confidence of having accomplished a tiresome labor is immense.

—Arnold Bennett

608

那些不能付諸實行的慾望，將會自壓抑中孳生病疫。

—— 威廉‧布萊克（英國詩人、畫家，1757-1827）

He who desires but acts not, breeds pestilence.

—William Blake

609

一位藝術家不能沒有天賦，而天賦則不能沒有努力的輔助。

—— 埃米爾‧左拉（法國小說家、劇作家，1840-1902）

The artist is nothing without the gift, but the gift is nothing without work.

—Émile Zola

610

上帝賦予了我們記憶，所以我們能夠在冬天也感受到玫瑰的花香。

—— 詹姆斯・馬修・巴里爵士（英國作家，1860－1937）

God gave us our memories so that we might have roses in December.
—Sir James Matthew Barrie

611

沒有哪一位藝術家是超越了當代。他所代表的就是他的時代，只不過其他人都還活在過去罷了。

—— 瑪莎・葛蘭姆（美國舞蹈家、編舞家，1894－1991）

No artist is ahead of his time. He is his time. It is just that the others are behind the time.
—Martha Graham

612

後浪推前浪：所以你無法再次踏入同樣的河流中。

—— 赫拉克利特（古希臘哲學家，535－475 B. C. ）

You can never step into the same river twice; for new waters are always flowing on to you.
—Heraclitus

613

增一分太多，減一分太少，這就是所謂完美的
境界。

—— 約瑟‧儒貝爾（法國道德學家、散文家，1754-1824）

A work is perfectly finished only when nothing can be added to it and
nothing taken away.　　　　　　　　　　　　　—Joseph Joubert

614

古之慎言人也，戒之哉！無多言，多言多敗。

—— 孔子（中國哲學家，551-479 B.C.）

Silence is the true friend that never betrays.　　　　　　—Confucius

615

文字的誤用總是會引發思想上的誤導。

—— 赫伯特‧史賓賽（英國哲學家，1820-1903）

How often misused words generate misleading thoughts.

—Herbert Spencer

616

當一位有耐心的人發火時，你可要小心了。

—— 約翰·德萊頓（英國詩人，1631-1700）

Beware the fury of a patient man!　　　　　—John Dryden

617

一艘待在港口裡的船無疑是安全的。但這並非是它被建造出來的目的。

—— 約翰·A·謝德（美國教育家，1859-1928）

A ship in harbor is safe, but that is not what ships are built for.
　　　　　　　　　　　　　　　　—John A. Shedd

618

兩犬相爭，勝負的關鍵並不一定在於體型的大小，而是在於其心中鬥志是否旺盛。

—— 德懷特·艾森豪（美國第三十四任總統，1890-1969）

What counts is not necessarily the size of the dog in the fight—it's the size of the fight in the dog.
　　　　　　　　　　　　　　　—Dwight D. Eisenhower

619

要像那驚濤駭浪不斷拍打的岬角一樣，堅忍地挺立於眾水的憤怒之中，不屈不撓。

——馬可·奧里略（羅馬皇帝、哲學家，121-180 A. D. ）

Be like the promotory against which the waves continually break, but it stands firm and tames the fury of the water around it.

——Marcus Aurelius

620

切莫將「移動」與「行動」混為一談。

——厄尼斯特·海明威（美國作家，1899-1961）

Never mistake motion for action.　　　　——Ernest Hemingway

621

做好一件事情所得到的獎勵，就在於完成這件事本身。

——拉爾夫·沃爾多·愛默生
（美國哲學家、詩人，1803-1882）

The reward of a thing well done is to have done it.

——Ralph Waldo Emerson

622

建議就好似雪花一般。越輕柔地著地，就越能
持久，也越能夠深深觸動人心。

—— 塞繆爾・泰勒・柯勒律治（英國詩人，1772-1834）

Advice is like snow; the softer it falls the longer it dwells upon, and the
deeper it sinks into the mind.　　　　　—Samuel Taylor Coleridge

623

你並不需要一位氣象專家來告訴你風現在正往
哪邊吹。

—— 巴布・狄倫（美國歌手、作詞家，1941-）

You don't need a weather man / To know which way the wind blows.
　　　　　　　　　　　　　　　　　　—Bob Dylan

624

縱然是至親至愛之人，也不能輕易相信。

—— 佚名

You trust your mother, but you cut the cards.

　　　　　　　　　　—Anonymous

625

在你登上一座山頂之後，依舊有其他高峰等著
你去攀爬。

—— 禪學諺語

When you reach the top, keep climbing.　　　　—Zen aphorism

626

藉由旁觀，你就能夠察覺到許多事。

—— 尤吉・貝拉（前美國大聯盟棒球員，1925–2015）

You can observe a lot just by watching.　　　　—Yogi Berra

627

演講的三個訣竅在於：真誠、簡潔、端正。

—— 富蘭克林・D・羅斯福
（美國第三十二任總統，1882–1945）

Hints on speech-making: be sincere . . . be brief . . . be seated.
—Franklin Delano Roosevelt

628

你必須要先發制人並且掌握全局。而主宰勝負的關鍵就在於自信。

—— 克莉絲・艾芙特（美國職業網球選手，1954-）

You've got to take the initiative and play your game. In a decisive set, confidence is the difference.
　　　　　　　　　　　　　　　　　　　—Chris Evert

629

鱈魚一次產下數以萬計的卵，而母雞一次不過下一顆蛋。但鱈魚並不像母雞一樣高聲啼叫，告訴你牠完成了什麼事。所以人們只讚揚母雞而無視鱈魚。這件事告訴我們，宣傳與行銷的重要。

—— 佚名

The codfish lays ten thousand eggs, the homely hen lays one. / The codfish never cackles to tell you what she's done. / And so we scorn the codfish, while the humble hen we prize, / which only goes to show you that it pays to advertise.
　　　　　　　　　　　　　　　　　　　—Anonymous

630

所有人類的智慧都可以濃縮於兩個詞：等待與
希望。

—— 大仲馬（法國小說家，1802-1870）

All human wisdom is summed up in two words—wait and hope.
　　　　　　　　　　　　　　　　　　—Alexandre Dumas

631

時常開懷大笑；贏得智者的尊敬與孩童的敬愛；
對於真誠的批評心懷感激，對虛偽朋友的背叛
淡然處之；欣賞美感，並看到人們最好的一面；
試著去改善這個世界：無論是藉由照顧好一個
孩子的健康，或修整花草，或其他使社會現況
更好的舉措。倘若有任何一個生命因為你的存
在而變得更美好，那就是成功的意義。

—— 拉爾夫・沃爾多・愛默生
（美國哲學家、詩人，1803-1882）

To laugh often and much; to win the respect of intelligent people and
the affection of children; to earn the appreciation of honest critics and
endure the betrayal of false friends; to appreciate beauty, to find the best
in others; to leave the world a little better; whether by a healthy child, a
garden patch or a redeemed social condition; to know even one life has
breathed easier because you have lived. This is the meaning of success.
　　　　　　　　　　　　　　　　　　—Ralph Waldo Emerson

第四章
心靈生命

CHAPTER 4
The Life of the Mind

632

我思故我在。

——勒內·笛卡兒
（法國哲學家、數學家，1596－1650）

Cogito ergo sum. (I think, therefore I am.) ——René Descartes

633

在這世上比千軍萬馬都還強大的，就是引領時代的思想。

——維克多·雨果
（法國小說家、詩人、劇作家，1802－1885）

Nothing else in the world . . . not all the armies . . . is so powerful as an idea whose time has come. ——Victor Hugo

634

思想形塑了我們；我們終將成為我們所想的樣貌。

——釋迦牟尼（佛教創始者，563－483 B. C. ）

We are shaped by our thoughts. We become what we think.
——Buddha

635

我願謙卑地向一隻鳥兒學習如何歌唱，也不願狂妄地去規範天上繁星該如何閃動。

——E·E·卡明斯（美國詩人，1894-1962）

I'd rather learn from one bird how to sing than to teach ten thousand stars how not to dance.　　　　——E. E. Cummings

636

想像力乃是能奏出道德美善的偉大樂器。

—— 雪萊（英國詩人，1792-1822）

The great instrument of moral good is the imagination.
　　　　——Percy Bysshe Shelley

637

驚嘆與好奇，是一切知識的開端。

——何塞·奧特嘉·伊·加塞特（西班牙作家，1883-1955）

To be surprised, to wonder, is to begin to understand.
　　　　——José Ortega y Gasset

638
知識就是力量。

—— 法蘭西斯·培根爵士
（英國哲學家、散文作家，1561-1626）

Knowledge is power.

—Sir Francis Bacon

639
跟一個無知的人爭辯是毫無意義的。

—— 威廉·G·麥卡杜
（美國政治家、前財政部長，1863-1941）

It is impossible to defeat an ignorant man in argument.

—William G. McAdoo

640
我之所以是世上最睿智的人，是因為我能夠理解自己的無知。

—— 蘇格拉底（古希臘哲學家，469-399 B. C.）

I am the wisest man alive, for I know one thing, and that is that I know nothing.

—Socrates

641

知識能夠被傳遞，但智慧卻不是那麼一回事。
我們能夠尋得智慧，並在生活中體認到它，或
者在奇蹟之中見識到它的存在。但是我們無法
以語言表達或教導智慧。

—— 赫曼・赫塞（德國詩人、小說家，1877-1962）

Knowledge can be conveyed, but not wisdom. It can be found, it can be
lived, it is possible to be carried by it, miracles can be performed with it,
but it cannot be expressed in words and taught.

—Herman Hesse

642

懷疑乃是智識的節操，切莫過早地放棄懷疑。
能夠在年輕的歲月中冷靜且自傲地保持著懷疑
的態度，是很可貴的。而直到心性成熟之時，
懷疑能夠安然地轉化成信仰與幸福。

—— 喬治・桑塔亞那（美國哲學家、詩人，1863-1952）

Skepticism is the chastity of the intellect, and it is shameful to surrender
it too soon or to the first comer: there is nobility in preserving it coolly
and proudly through long youth, until at last, in the ripeness of instinct
and discretion, it can be safely exchanged for fidelity and happiness.

—George Santayana

643

我踏著前人的腳步走到了現在的境界。我所閱讀的乃是數個世代的先人所撰寫的書籍。我是他們所經歷的體驗與冒險的總和，而你也應該如此。

—— 艾利・魏瑟爾（美國猶太裔作家，1928–2016）

Others have been here before me, and I walk in their footsteps. The books I have read were composed by generations of fathers and sons, mothers and daughters, teachers and disciples. I am the sum total of their experiences, their quests. And so are you.

—Elie Wiesel

644

如果我們重視對於知識的追求，我們必須能夠全然自由地讓知識引領我們。自由的心靈不能像被鐵鍊拴著腳的狗一樣受到束縛。

—— 狄奧多・阿多諾（德國哲學家、社會學家，1903–1969）

If we value the pursuit of knowledge, we must be free to follow wherever that search may lead us. The free mind is no barking dog to be tethered on a one-foot chain.

—Theodor Adorno

645

如何能同時在心中保有互相衝突的思想，但又能夠順利思考，這就是第一流知識份子所面臨的考驗。舉例來說，他必須要能夠看透這世上一切事物都是毫無希望，但又能下定決心去改變這樣的現狀。

——F・史考特・費茲傑羅（美國小說家，1896-1940）

The test of a first-rate intelligence is the ability to hold two opposed ideas in the mind at the same time, and still retain the ability to function. One should, for example, be able to see that things are hopeless and yet be determined to make them otherwise. ——F. Scott Fitzgerald

646

一個受過教育的心靈，能夠懷抱一種思想，但並非全然接受它。

—— 亞里斯多德（希臘哲學家，384-322 B.C.）

It is the mark of an educated mind to be able to entertain a thought without accepting it. ——Aristotle

647

幽默是一件嚴肅的事。我認為它是人類天性中最偉大的特質，應該被永恆保存。

—— 詹姆斯·瑟伯（美國作家、漫畫家，1894–1961）

Humor is a serious thing. I like to think of it as one of our greatest earliest natural resources, which must be preserved at all cost.

—James Thurber

648

在你閱讀經典的時候，你並非是從書中看到了你之前從未見過的事物，而是在你自己心中看到了一個全新的自己。

—— 克里夫頓·費迪曼（美國文學評論家，1904–1999）

When you read a classic you do not see in the book more than you did before. You see more in you than there was before.

—Clifton Fadiman

649

平庸之人難以有超越自己的眼界，而有才之人能夠瞬間看出別人的天才之處。

—— 亞瑟・柯南・道爾爵士（英國作家，1859－1930）

Mediocrity knows nothing higher than itself, but talent instantly recognizes genius.
　　　　　　　　　　　　　　　　—Sir Arthur Conan Doyle

650

生活能夠打擊甚至壓垮靈魂，而藝術則是提醒我們，我們依舊擁有著靈魂。

—— 史黛拉・艾德勒（美國舞台劇演員，1901－1992）

Life beats down and crushes the soul, but art reminds you that you have one.
　　　　　　　　　　　　　　　　　　　—Stella Adler

651

上帝賜與了我們感知、理性與智慧。我相信他並不希望我們放棄運用這些天賦。

—— 伽利略・伽利萊
（義大利物理學家、天文學家、數學家、哲學家，1564－1642）

I do not feel obliged to believe that that same God who has endowed us with sense, reason, and intellect has intended us to forego their use.
　　　　　　　　　　　　　　　　　　　—Galileo Galilei

652

充盈滿溢乃是美。

—— 威廉·布萊克（英國詩人、畫家，1757-1827）

Exuberance is beauty.　　　　　　　　　　　　—William Blake

653

寫作乃是與沈默的艱苦對抗。

—— 卡洛斯·富恩特斯（墨西哥作家，1928-2012）

Writing is a struggle against silence.　　　　　　　—Carlos Fuentes

654

跟一個愚人講道理，他反而會認為你是個蠢蛋。

—— 歐里庇得斯（希臘劇作家，480-406 B.C.）

Talk sense to a fool and he calls you foolish.　　　　—Euripides

655

教育並非只是將知識灌輸給學生，而是能一瞬間點亮人們心靈的光焰。

—— 威廉·巴特勒·葉慈（愛爾蘭詩人，1865-1939）

Education is not the filling of a pail, but the lighting of a fire.

—William Butler Yeats

656

你無法教導一個人任何事，你只能夠幫助他，讓他自己領悟。

—— 伽利略·伽利萊
（義大利物理學家、天文學家、數學家、哲學家，1564-1642）

You cannot teach a man anything; you can only help him find it within himself.

—Galileo Galilei

657

一個人的行動就是其思想的最佳詮釋。

—— 約翰·洛克（英國實證主義哲學家，1632-1704）

I have always thought the actions of men the best interpreters of their thoughts.

—John Locke

658

也許教育的最佳成果，就是無論喜惡都能夠克
盡職責的能力。

—— 沃爾特‧白芝浩（英國經濟學家、散文家，1826-1877）

Perhaps the most valuable result of all education is the ability to make
yourself do the thing you have to do, when it ought to be done, whether
you like it or not. —Walter Bagehot

659

人們主張言論自由，但是事實上他們卻連自由
地思考都無法做到。

—— 索倫‧齊克果（丹麥哲學家，1813-1855）

People demand freedom of speech to make up for the freedom of
thought which they avoid. —Søren Kierkegaard

660

那些引用權威人士的話語來爭論的人，運用的
不是自己的智慧，而不過是記憶罷了。

—— 李奧納多‧達文西
（義大利藝術家、發明家，1492-1519）

Anyone who conducts an argument by appealing to authority is not
using his intelligence; he is just using his memory.

—Leonardo da Vinci

661

當我花了這麼多時間來說服自己，自己做的事是對的，難道不是因為：我已經隱約認知到我可能是錯的嗎？

—— 珍·奧斯汀（英國小說家，1775-1817）

Where so many hours have been spent in convincing myself that I am right, is there not some reason to fear I may be wrong?

—Jane Austen

662

那些從未受過教育之水灌溉的心靈，將會孳生偏見，就好像在亂石間叢生的雜草一樣，難以拔除。

—— 夏綠蒂·勃朗特（英國小說家，1816-1855）

Prejudices, it is well known, are most difficult to eradicate from the heart whose soil has never been loosened or fertilized by education; they grow there, firm as weeds among rocks.

—Charlotte Brontë

663

人類教育的用意在於，在鍛鍊心靈的同時得到樂趣。

—— 賈奎‧巴祖恩（法裔美國歷史學家，1907-2012）

The test and the use of man's education is that he finds pleasure in the exercise of his mind. ——Jacques Martin Barzun

664

我發現有許多的資訊都是無意中得到的；我尋找著某樣事物，但是在這個過程中，我發現了其它意想不到的驚喜。

—— 法蘭克林‧亞當斯（美國專欄作家，1881-1960）

I find that a great part of the information I have was acquired by looking up something and finding something else on the way.

——Franklin P. Adams

665

作家所渴望的不是尊敬、讚揚或熱愛，而是理解。這也許就是作家異於其他職業的獨特之處。

—— 李歐‧C‧羅斯丹（美國作家，1908-1997）

The writer wants to be understood much more than he wants to be respected or praised or even loved. And that perhaps, is what makes him different from others. ——Leo C. Rosten

666

幻想，倘若不能以理性相輔，將會產生難以想像的恐怖怪物。而如果兩者相輔相成，就能夠孕育出奇蹟般的藝術。

——哥雅（西班牙畫家，1746-1828）

Fantasy, abandoned by reason, produces impossible monsters; united with it, she is the mother of the arts and the origin of marvels.

—Francisco de Goya

667

這也許聽起來有些矛盾，但是事實上，人生總是在模仿藝術，而非藝術模仿人生。

——奧斯卡·王爾德（愛爾蘭文學家，1854-1900）

Paradoxically though it may seem, it is none the less true that life imitates art far more than art imitates life. —Oscar Wilde

668

所謂天才，不過是對保持耐心有著極高的天賦。

——喬治路易·布豐伯爵
（法國數學家、生物學家，1707-1788）

Genius is nothing but a great aptitude for patience.

—George-Louis de Buffon

669

當人們廝混在一起時，是最無趣且俗不可耐的。
唯有孤獨才能夠創造令人耳目一新的獨特性。

—— 安迪・沃荷（美國普普藝術家，1928-1987）

People are always so boring when they band together. You have to be alone to develop all the idiosyncrasies that make a person interesting.

—Andy Warhol

670

有創造性的心靈，能夠通過任何嚴酷的試煉。

—— 安娜・佛洛伊德（英國精神分析師，1895-1982）

Creative minds have been known to survive any sort of bad training.

—Anna Freud

671

知識份子用複雜的方式講述一件簡單的事情；
藝術家則是以簡單的方式呈現複雜的事物。

—— 查理・布考斯基（德裔美國小說家、詩人，1920-1994）

An intellectual is a man who says a simple thing in a difficult way; an artist is a man who says a difficult thing in a simple way.

—Charles Bukowski

672

概念，或所謂的基礎心靈活動，乃是藝術不可或缺的要素。藝術家的職責就在於深化那些世人覺得神秘的事物。

——法蘭西斯·培根爵士
（英國哲學家、散文作家，1561-1626）

Conception, my boy, fundamental brain work, is what makes all the difference in art. The job of the artist is always to deepen the mystery.
—Francis Bacon

673

藝術的目的是撩動人心，科學則是安定人心。那些無法解釋的事物，就是藝術的唯一價值。

——喬治·布拉克（法國畫家，1882-1963）

Art is made to disturb. Science reassures. There is only one valuable thing in art: the thing you cannot explain.　　　—Georges Braque

674

所謂「精確無誤」並不存在於現實中。

——亨利·馬諦斯（法國畫家、雕塑家，1869-1954）

Precision is not reality.　　　—Henri Matisse

675

生命短促，藝術長存。

——希波克拉底（古希臘醫學家，460-370 B.C.）

Life is brief, art is long.   —Hippocrates

676

藝術的目的在於揭露那些被既定答案所掩蓋的
真理。

——詹姆斯·鮑德溫（美國作家、評論家，1924-1987）

The purpose of art is to lay bare the questions which have been hidden
by the answers.   —James Baldwin

677

真正的智慧有著一個永恆不變的特色：那就是
能夠在尋常的事物中看見不凡。

——拉爾夫·沃爾多·愛默生
（美國哲學家、詩人，1803-1882）

The invariable mark of wisdom is to see the miraculous in the common.
—Ralph Waldo Emerson

678

學徒倘若不能青出於藍而勝於藍，殆矣！

—— 李奧納多·達文西
（義大利藝術家、發明家，1492-1519）

Poor is the pupil who does not surpass his master.

—Leonardo da Vinci

679

上帝呀，請讓我永遠地渴望那些我能力之外的事物吧。

—— 米開朗基羅（義大利文藝復興時期藝術家，1475-1564）

Lord, grant that I may always desire more than I can accomplish.

—Michelangelo

680

創意會使你犯下一些錯誤，而藝術則是讓你知道，哪些錯誤是值得保存的。

—— 史考特·亞當斯（美國諷刺漫畫家，1957-）

Creativity is allowing yourself to make mistakes. Art is knowing which ones to keep.

—Scott Adams

681

在每個人內心深處都有能與美感產生共鳴的地方。

—— 克里斯多福·達林頓·莫里
（美國作家、編輯，1890－1957）

In every man's heart there is a secret nerve that answers to the vibrations of beauty. —Christopher Darlington Morley

682

事物本身並無美感，美感存在於能靜觀的人心中。

—— 大衛·休謨（蘇格蘭哲學家，1711－1776）

Beauty in things lies in the mind which contemplates them.
—David Hume

683

人生中最美麗的事物無法以肉眼看見，也無法以手觸及。而是必須用心體會。

—— 海倫·凱勒（美國作家、社會運動家、講師，1880－1968）

The best and most beautiful things in life cannot be seen, not touched, but are felt in the heart. —Helen Keller

684

倘若人能夠駐足靜觀，就會發現隨處皆有花朵盛開。

—— 亨利・馬諦斯（法國畫家、雕塑家，1869-1954）

There are flowers everywhere, for those who bother to look.

—Henri Matisse

685

上帝呀，請賜與我優雅的態度，去接受那些無法被改變的事物。也請賜與我勇氣去改變那些應該被改變的。最後，請賜與我智慧來明辨以上兩者。

—— 雷因霍爾德・尼布爾（美國神學家，1892-1971）

God, give us the grace to accept with serenity the things that cannot be changed, courage to change the things which should be changed, and the wisdom to distinguish the one from the other.

—Reinhold Niebuhr

686

別以冗言贅字描述簡單的事，而是以簡單的言語表達豐富的意涵。

—— 畢達哥拉斯（古希臘哲學家、數學家，580－500 B.C.）

Do not say a little in many words but a great deal in a few.

—Pythagorus

687

教育之於靈魂，就好像雕刻家之於一顆未經琢磨的大理石。

—— 約瑟夫·艾迪生
（英國散文家、詩人、政治家，1672－1719）

What sculpture is to a block of marble, education is to the soul.

—Joseph Addison

688

真正的教育，應該能夠引領我們走出封閉的自我，進入更高深的境界：那就是能夠與全人類緊密結合的無私精神。

—— 南希·阿斯特夫人（英國政治家，1879－1964）

Real education should educate us out of self into something far finer; into a selflessness which links us with all humanity.

—Lady Nancy Astor

689

教育的意義，就是要去除一個人的奴性。

—— 菲德利克·道格拉斯

（美國廢奴主義作家、演說家，1818-1895）

To educate a man is to unfit him to be a slave.

—Fredrick Douglass

690

只要有著上帝與好書的陪伴，沒有人能夠說他是孤獨的。

—— 伊麗莎白·巴雷特·白朗寧（英國詩人，1806-1861）

No man can be called friendless when he has God and the companionship of good books.

—Elizabeth Barrett Browning

691

藉由語言與文字，心靈就能夠展翅翱翔。

—— 阿里斯托芬（古希臘劇作家，448-388 B.C.）

By words the mind is winged.

—Aristophanes

692

睿智的人說話，是因為他有話要說；而愚蠢的人說話，只是因為他覺得自己得說些什麼。

—— 索爾·貝婁（美國小說家，1915-2005）

Wise men talk because they have something to say; fools talk because they have to say something.　　　　—Saul Bellow

693

一知半解則危矣；若欲飲知識之泉，切不可淺嘗而止。

—— 亞歷山大·波普（英國詩人、諷刺文學家，1688-1744）

A little learning is a dangerous thing / Drink deep, or taste not the Pierian spring.　　　　—Alexander Pope

694

切莫成為語言和文字的奴隸。

—— 湯瑪斯·卡萊爾（英國歷史學家，1795-1881）

Be not a slave of words.　　　　—Thomas Carlyle

695

無知者的自信，能勝過智者的猶豫不決。

——佚名

The confidence of ignorance will always overcome indecision of knowledge.　　　　　　——Anonymous

696

缺乏智慧的正直，乃是軟弱且無用的。而缺乏了正直的智慧，則是危險且可怖的。

——塞繆爾・詹森（英國作家，1709－1784）

Integrity without knowledge is weak and useless, and knowledge without integrity is dangerous and dreadful.

——Samuel Johnson

697

那些致志於習得知識的人，都願意付出任何代價。

——尤維納利斯（羅馬詩人，約活躍於西元一到二世紀）

All wish to possess knowledge, but few, comparatively speaking, are willing to pay the price.　　　　　　——Juvenal

698

真正的智慧總是持保留的態度。智者時常懷疑並改變想法；而愚者則是固執己見，從不懷疑。愚者千知萬知，但卻無法知道自己的無知。

—— 阿肯那頓（古埃及第十八王朝法老，-1354 B. C.）

True wisdom is less presuming than folly. The wise man doubteth often, and changeth his mind; the fool is obstinate, and doubteth not; he knoweth all things but his own ignorance.

—Akhenaton

699

一本真正讓你折服的好書，是會讓你在讀完之後，希望作者是一位能夠隨時談心的好朋友。但這實在是很少見的情況。

—— J·D·沙林傑（美國小說家，1919-2010）

What really knocks me out is a book that, when you're all done reading it, you wish the author that wrote it was a terrific friend of yours and you could call him up on the phone whenever you felt like it. That doesn't happen much, though.

—J. D. Salinger

700

一個民族的獨特藝術，乃是其心靈的最真實寫照。

—— 賈瓦哈拉爾·尼赫魯（印度第一任總理，1889－1964）

The art of a people is a true mirror to their minds.

—Jawaharlal Nehru

701

縱然是天才也有其侷限之處，但是愚蠢卻是沒有極限的。

—— L·羅恩·賀伯特
（美國作家、山達基教創始人，1911－1986）

Genius may have its limitations, but stupidity is not thus handicapped.

—L. Ron Hubbard

702

處心積慮想要復仇的人，只會讓自己的傷痕更難痊癒。能放下仇恨的人，才能夠真正活得快樂。

—— 約翰·米爾頓（英國詩人，1608－1674）

He that studieth revenge keepeth his own wounds green, which otherwise would heal and do well.

—John Milton

703

第一位以辱罵代替暴力的人，就是人類文明的
創始者。

—— 席格蒙・佛洛伊德（奧地利精神分析師，1856-1939）

The first man to use abusive language instead of his fists was the founder
of civilization. ——Sigmund Freud

704

當心那些只讀通一本書的人。＊

—— 聖多瑪斯・阿奎納
（義大利哲學家、神學家，1225-1274）

Beware the man of a single book. ——St. Thomas Aquinas

＊ 本句（拉丁原文 Hominem unius libri temo）有兩種詮釋：第一種是表
達對某些知識領域專精者的敬畏之情，第二種是諷刺那些讀書
不多的愚人。

705

智慧需要以智慧來理解；倘若聽眾皆為耳聾之輩，音樂也就毫無意義。

——沃爾特・李普曼（美國記者，1889-1974）

It requires wisdom to understand wisdom; the music is nothing if the audience is deaf.
　　　　　　　　　　　　　　　　　　　　——Walter Lippman

706

那些能夠打破心靈的枷鎖，從此停止憂煩操心的人們，能夠得到永遠的喜樂。

——奧維德（羅馬詩人，43 B.C.-17 A.D.）

Happy the man who has broken the chains which hurt the mind, and has given up worrying, once and for all.　　　　　——Ovid

707

人類的歷史，已經演變為教育和災禍之間的競逐。

——H・G・威爾斯（英國作家，1866-1946）

Human history becomes more and more a race between education and catastrophe.　　　　　　　　　　　——H. G. Wells

708

所謂的天才之資，不過是見解深刻的常識罷了。

—— 喬許・畢林斯（美國散文家，1818-1885）

Genius ain't anything more than elegant common sense.

—Josh Billings

709

以常識因應情勢而為，乃是盡忠職守的最佳智慧與哲學。面對世事，應坦然且謙卑地接受命運、祝福那些帶給我們喜樂的人、並且棄絕虛偽與造作。

—— 賀拉斯・華爾波（英國作家，1717-1797）

To act with common sense, according to the moment, is the best wisdom I know and the best philosophy is to do one's duties, take the world as it comes, submit respectfully to one's lot; bless the goodness that has given us so much happiness with it, whatever it is; and despise affectation.

—Horace Walpole

710

如果你讓某人覺得自己有些獨特的想法，他會喜歡與你為友。但如果你要他真正地去動腦思考，他可能會對你感到厭煩。

—— 唐納‧羅伯特‧佩里‧瑪奇
（美國記者、幽默作家，1878－1937）

If you make people think they're thinking, they'll love you; but if you really make them think, they'll hate you.

—Donald Robert Perry Marquis

711

不恥下問的人，馬上就會脫離愚昧，而從不開口問的人，則會持續愚昧一輩子。

—— 馬克‧吐溫（美國作家，1835－1910）

He who asks is a fool for five minutes, but he who does not ask remains a fool forever.

—Mark Twain

712

一位懂得聆聽的人，不只會到處受人喜愛。透過聆聽，他自己也能夠學到許多事物。

—— 威爾遜‧米茲納（美國劇作家，1876－1933）

A good listener is not only popular everywhere, but after a while he gets to know something.

—Wilson Mizner

713

教育能夠使一個民族遵從領導，但並非被盲目驅使；受過教育的民族能接受政府治理，但絕不會被奴役。

—— 亨利·布洛漢勳爵（英國政治家，1778-1868）

Education makes a people easy to lead, but difficult to drive; easy to govern but impossible to enslave. —Lord Henry Brougham

714

一個正確的答案，就好似一個深情的吻。

—— 歌德（德國戲劇家、詩人，1749-1832）

A correct answer is like an affectionate kiss.

—Johann Wolfgang von Goethe

715

智慧不是管教所能產生的，而是要透過一生的努力去學得。

—— 愛因斯坦（猶太裔美國物理學家，1879-1955）

Wisdom is not a product of schooling but of the lifelong attempt to acquire it. —Albert Einstein

716

一名教師的感染力是永恒的；他永遠無法得知他的影響在何處終止。

　　　　　　　　　—— 亨利・布魯克斯・亞當斯
　　　　　　　　　（美國歷史學家、作家，1838－1918）

A teacher affects eternity; he can never tell, where his influence stops.
　　　　　　　　　　　　—Henry Brooks Adams

717

教導別人，對於自己也是再次學習的機會。

　　—— 約瑟・儒貝爾（法國道德學家、散文家，1754－1824）

To teach is to learn twice.
　　　　　　　　　　　　—Joseph Joubert

718

切莫湮滅你的靈感與想像力；也切莫成為既定形式的奴隸。

　　　　　　　　　—— 文森・梵谷（荷蘭畫家，1853－1890）

Do not quench your inspiration and your imagination; do not become
the slave of your model.　　　　　　—Vincent van Gogh

719

獨特的風格能夠化繁為簡，也能夠化簡為繁。

——尚・考克多

（法國詩人、小說家、劇作家、導演，1889-1963）

Style can make complicated things seem simple, or simple things complicated. ——Jean Cocteau

720

世界的風潮總是不斷轉變，但是一個人的風格是亙古不變的。

——佚名

Fashions change, but style is forever. ——Anonymous

721

我們必須審慎地從經驗中習得智慧，但不能受到經驗的侷限。否則，我們就會像一隻被熱爐所燙著的貓，牠從經驗中學到不再坐在任何爐蓋上，即便那個爐子是冰冷且安全的。

—— 馬克・吐溫（美國作家，1835-1910）

We should be careful to get out of an experience only the wisdom that is in it—and stop there; lest we be like the cat that sits down on a hot stove-lid. She will never sit down on a hot stove-lid again—and that is well; but also she will never sit down on a cold one anymore.

—Mark Twain

722

科學研究中的每一個真相，都可以成為下一個知識的假設前提。

—— 康拉德・羅倫茲（奧地利動物學家，1903-1989）

Truth in science can be defined as the working hypothesis best suited to open the way to the next better one.

—Konrad Lorenz

723

常識與規範的存在，使我們免於思考的勞苦。

—— 約翰·肯尼斯·加爾布雷斯
（美國經濟學家，1908－2006）

The conventional view serves to protect us from the painful job of thinking. —John Kenneth Galbraith

724

有些人總會愚蠢地以為，以強勢的態度說話，就代表他懂得比別人要多。

—— 赫爾曼·梅爾維爾（美國作家，1819－1891）

A man thinks that by mouthing hard words he understands hard things. —Herman Melville

725

心靈自在其位，一動念間能使天堂成地獄、地獄成天堂。

—— 約翰·米爾頓（英國詩人，1608－1674）

The mind is its own place, and in itself, can make heaven of Hell, and a hell of Heaven. —John Milton

726

我引用旁人的話語，只為了能夠更透徹地表達自己。

—— 米歇爾・德・蒙田（法國散文家，1533-1592）

I quote others only in order the better to express myself.
—Michel de Montaigne

727

若能保持開闊的心胸與昂揚的鬥志，縱使犯下了些許錯誤，也比眼界狹隘、畏首畏尾的人要好得多。

—— 文森・梵谷（荷蘭畫家，1853-1890）

It is better to be high-spirited even though one makes more mistakes, than to be narrow-minded and too prudent.
—Vincent van Gogh

728

詩歌自愉悅而始，以智慧作結。
—— 羅伯特・佛洛斯特（美國詩人，1874-1963）

Poetry begins in delight and ends in wisdom.
—Robert Frost

729

兩個在今天意見相左而激烈爭吵的人，到了明天可能又變得同仇敵愾。

—— 克里斯多福・達林頓・莫里
（美國作家、編輯，1890-1957）

There is no squabbling so violent as that between people who accepted
an idea yesterday and those who will accept the same idea tomorrow.

—Christopher Darlington Morley

730

好的記性從來就不代表智慧。這就好比一本字典跟一部論著，其等級天差地遠。

—— 約翰・亨利・紐曼（英國神學家，1801-1890）

A great memory is never made synonymous with wisdom, any more
than a dictionary would be called a treatise.

—John Henry Newman

731

低頭俯視自身的處境，往往比揚首眺望遠處還要更接近智慧。

—— 威廉・華滋華斯（英國浪漫主義詩人，1770-1850）

Wisdom is ofttimes nearer when we stoop / Than when we soar.

—William Wordsworth

732

真正的智慧乃是：巧手雕琢璞玉，妙語道盡人事。

—— 亞歷山大·波普（英國詩人、諷刺文學家，1688-1744）

True wit is nature to advantage dressed, / What oft was thought, but ne'er so well expressed.　　　　　　　　　　—Alexander Pope

733

未受過教育的人，最好能夠讀讀收錄名言佳句的書籍。《巴特雷特名言錄》是一本我潛心閱讀過的好書。那些刻印在記憶上的名言給予你靈感，也啟發你去閱讀更多偉大的著作。

—— 溫斯頓·邱吉爾（前英國首相，1874-1965）

It is a good thing for an uneducated man to read books of quotations. *Bartlett's Familiar Quotations* is an admirable work, and I studied it intently. The quotations when engraved upon the memory give you good thoughts. They also make you anxious to read the authors and look for more.　　　　　　　　　　—Sir Winston Churchill

734

幾乎每一句至理名言，都會伴隨著另一句與其
意見相左、但也同樣富有智慧的名言。

—— 喬治・桑塔亞那（美國哲學家、詩人，1863－1952）

Almost every wise saying has an opposite one, no less wise, to balance it.
　　　　　　　　　　　　　　　　　　—George Santayana

735

你所認為的「荒謬」，不過就是與你的意見截
然不同的想法罷了。

—— 安布洛斯・畢爾斯（美國記者，1842－1914）

Absurdity, n.: A statement or belief manifestly inconsistent with one's
own opinion.　　　　　　　　　　　　　　　—Ambrose Bierce

736

愚者默然思忖；智者不恥下問。

—— 班傑明・狄斯雷利（英國前首相、作家，1804－1881）

The fool wonders, the wise man asks.　　　　　　—Benjamin Disraeli

737

抱怨只會如回音一般，從世界的另一端反射回來。而沈默卻能夠使我們更堅強。

——G·K·卻斯特頓（英國作家，1874-1936）

Complaint always comes back in an echo from the ends of the world; but silence strengthens us.　　　　　　——G. K. Chesterton

738

誠心的懷疑，要比那些一知半解的信仰要包含了更多的信念。

——阿佛烈·丁尼生（英國詩人，1809-1892）

There lives more faith in honest doubt, believe me, than in half the creeds.　　　　　　——Alfred, Lord Tennyson

739

假使人們從未經歷過那些愚行所造成的苦果，這世上只會有更多的愚人。

——赫伯特·史賓賽（英國哲學家，1820-1903）

The ultimate result of shielding men from the effects of folly, is to fill the world with fools.　　　　　　——Herbert Spencer

740

對於一個說謊者的懲罰，不在於沒有人相信的他的話，而是在於他自己也已經無法相信任何人。

—— 蕭伯納（愛爾蘭劇作家、文學批評家，1856-1950）

The liar's punishment is not in the least that he is not believed, but that he cannot believe anyone else. —George Bernard Shaw

741

矛盾絕非是謬誤的徵象，而沒有矛盾也並不代表就是真實。

—— 帕斯卡（法國哲學家，1623-1662）

Contradiction is not a sign of falsity, nor the lack of contradiction a sign of truth. —Blaise Pascal

742

所謂積極正面的態度，不過是被別人高亢的論調所誤導罷了。

—— 安布洛斯·畢爾斯（美國記者，1842-1914）

To be positive: To be mistaken at the top of one's voice. —Ambrose Bierce

743

我不同意你所說的話，但是我誓死維護你說話的權利。

—— 伏爾泰（法國哲學家，1694-1778）

I do not agree with what you say, but I will defend to the death your right to say it.　　　　　　　　　　—Voltaire

744

對於那些終於從愚行中清醒過來的人，我不知道該憐憫還是恭喜他們。

—— 威廉·梅克比斯·薩克萊（英國小說家，1811-1863）

I never know whether to pity or congratulate a man on coming to his senses.　　　　　　　—William Makepeace Thackeray

745

有些已經消逝在人類記憶中的書籍，是不該被遺忘的；而那些已經流芳千古的書，都是值得被記住的。

——W·H·奧登（英裔美籍詩人，1907-1973）

Some books are undeservedly forgotten; none are undeservedly remembered.　　　　　　　　　　—W. H. Auden

746

道出真相的話語並不總是悅耳的；悅耳的話語
也不總是真實的。

—— 佚名

True words are not always pretty; pretty words are not always true.

—Anonymous

747

真理僅存在於細微之處，謬誤則是隨處可見。

—— 亨利‧聖約翰子爵（英國政治家、作家，1678-1751）

Truth lies within a little and certain compass, but error is immense.

—Henry St. John

748

別對謊言追根究底，它會自己走向毀滅。

—— 利曼‧比徹（美國長老教會牧師，1775-1863）

Never chase a lie. Let it alone, and it will run itself to death.

—Lyman Beecher

749

縱使是敵人，我們也能夠從他身上學到東西。

—— 阿里斯多芬（古希臘劇作家，448-388 B.C.）

A man may learn wisdom even from a foe.

—Aristophenes

750

一位年輕人將一個陳舊的想法當作是自己的創見，再也沒有比這更傲慢且可笑的事了。

—— 席德尼·哈里斯（美國漫畫家，活躍於二十世紀）

Nobody can be so amusingly arrogant as a young man who has just discovered an old idea and thinks it is his own.

—Sydney Harris

751

一個正確言論的反面，是一個謬誤的言論。一個深刻真理的反面，卻很可能是另一個深刻的真理。

—— 尼爾斯·波赫（丹麥物理學家，1885-1962）

The opposite of a correct statement is a false statement. The opposite of a profound truth may well be another profound truth.

—Niels Bohr

752

信仰之所以真實深刻，並非在於其實用價值。

—— 亨利·腓特烈·愛彌爾
（瑞士哲學家、詩人，1821-1881）

A belief is not true because it is useful. —Henri Frédéric Amiel

753

儘管真理稀如晨星，但對於人們，它永遠是供過於求。

—— 喬許·畢林斯（美國散文家，1818-1885）

As scarce as truth is, the supply has always been in excess of the demand.
—Josh Billings

754

對於昨日我深信不疑之事，到了今日我已有所懷疑；而到了明日，我也許也會懷疑我今日所深信之事。

—— 馬修·阿諾德（英國詩人、文學批評家，1822-1888）

I do not believe today everything I believed yesterday; I wonder will I believe tomorrow everything I believe today.
—Matthew Arnold

755

信仰不只是心靈所懷抱的想法，更是掌控了心靈的執念。

—— 羅伯特·歐克斯頓·波爾特
（英國劇作家，1924-1995）

A belief is not merely an idea the mind possesses; it is an idea that possesses the mind. ——Robert Oxton Bolt

756

神意藏在細節中。＊

—— 路德維希·密斯·凡德羅（德國建築師，1886-1969）

God is in the details.

——Ludwig Mies van der Rohe

＊ 較常見的「魔鬼藏在細節中」（The Devil is in the detail）就是從此句變化而來。同樣表達藝術創作中細節的重要性。

757

當一個人做出與其過去的言行相違背的事情時，如果你對他本就懷有好感，他就是個有勇氣順應情勢去做出改變的開明之人。而倘若你對他本就懷忿在心，他就成了食言而肥的卑鄙小人。

—— 法蘭克林·亞當斯（美國專欄作家，1881-1960）

When a man you like switches from what he said a year ago, or four years ago, he is a broad-minded person who has courage enough to change his mind with changing conditions. When a man you don't like does it, he is a liar who has broken his promises.

—Franklin P. Adams

758

在「真實」還未回過神來之前，「謊言」早已傳遍天下了。

—— 溫斯頓·邱吉爾（前英國首相，1874-1965）

A lie gets halfway around the world before the truth has a chance to get its pants on.

—Sir Winston Churchill

759

人類的理性，就好像馬背上的醉漢；剛從左邊
扶他上馬，他轉眼間就從右邊摔了下去。

—— 馬丁・路德（德國宗教改革領導者，1483－1546）

Human reason is like a drunken man on horseback; set it up on one side
and it tumbles over on the other.

—Martin Luther

760

我痛恨一成不變的想法。我認為藝術家總是要
能夠超越他的時代。

—— 奧森・威爾斯
（美國電影導演、編劇、演員，1915－1985）

I passionately hate the idea of being with it, I think an artist has always
to be out of step with his time. —Orson Welles

761

任何偉大的藝術作品都重現並改寫了時空。而
其偉大的程度端看它如何能使你感受到自身存
在於這個世界、並引領你進入那奇異且超脫世
俗的氛圍中。

——雷納德·伯恩斯坦（美國指揮家、作曲家，1918-1990）

Any great work of art revives and readapts time and space, and the
measure of its success is the extent to which it makes you an inhabitant
of that world—the extent to which it invites you in and lets you breathe
its strange, special air.   —Leonard Bernstein

762

那些在深夜裡，於自己心中灰暗角落做夢之人，
在早上醒來時只會哀嘆於世界的虛無。但那些
在白日中懷抱夢想之人是危險的；他們能夠將
所夢化為行動，進而在現實中將夢想化為可能。

——T·E·勞倫斯（英國考古學家、軍事將領、外交官、作家，
人稱「阿拉伯的勞倫斯」1888-1935）

Those who dream by night in the dusty recesses of their minds wake
in the day to find that all was vanity, but the dreamers of the day are
dangerous men for they may act their dream with open eyes and make
it possible.   —T. E. Lawrence

763

心懷惡意所道出的真言，比任何羅織的謊言還要惡毒。

—— 威廉·布萊克（英國詩人、畫家，1757-1827）

Truth that's told with bad intent / Beats all the Lies you can invent.
—William Blake

764

讓我遠離那些不知悲傷的智慧、不懂歡笑的哲理，以及不識孩童純真的自以為是。

—— 紀伯倫（黎巴嫩詩人，1883-1931）

Keep me away from the wisdom which does not cry, the philosophy which does not laugh, and the greatness which does not bow before children.
—Kahlil Gibran

765

人類的心靈一旦受到新想法的形塑，就很難恢復到原來的樣子。

—— 小奧利弗·溫德爾·霍姆斯
（美國法學家、最高法院大法官，1841-1935）

Man's mind, once stretched by a new idea, never regains its original dimensions.
—Oliver Wendell Holmes, Jr.

766

如果你要說的話對現狀毫無益處，那還是閉上嘴巴吧。

> ——豪爾赫·路易斯·波赫士
> （阿根廷作家、詩人、翻譯家，1899-1986）

Don't talk unless you can improve the silence.

> —Jorge Luis Borges

767

垃圾桶是作家最好的夥伴。

> ——艾薩克·巴甚維斯·辛格
> （美國猶太裔小說家，1902-1991）

The wastebasket is the writer's best friend.

> —Isaac Bashevis Singer

768

在追求知識時我們喪失了何等的智慧？而在接受資訊時我們又喪失了何等的知識？

> ——T·S·艾略特（英國詩人，1885-1968）

Where is the wisdom we have lost in knowledge? Where is the knowledge we have lost in information?　　　　—T. S. Eliot

769

不願講理之人，是為頑石；不能講理之人，是為愚者；不敢講理之人，是為奴才。

—— 喬治‧戈登‧拜倫勳爵
（英國詩人、革命家，1788－1824）

Those who will not reason are bigots, those who cannot are fools, and those who dare not are slaves. —George Gordon, Lord Byron

770

具備敏銳觀察力的人，時常被其他人視為憤世嫉俗。

—— 蕭伯納（愛爾蘭劇作家、文學批評家，1856－1950）

The power of accurate observation is commonly called cynicism by those who have not got it. —George Bernard Shaw

771

對一位藝術家來說，大自然中沒有任何事物是醜惡的。

—— 奧古斯特‧羅丹（法國雕刻家，1840－1917）

To the artist there is never anything ugly in nature.

—Auguste Rodin

772

縱使是在荒蕪寂寥之處，繁星依舊閃耀。

——佚名

Even in the desolate wilderness, stars can still shine.

—Anonymous

773

和平並不只是國與國之間的關係，也不僅僅是代表沒有戰爭。它也是一種從靈魂的平靜中產生的心靈狀態。唯有心靈平靜的民族，才能夠擁有長久的和平。

—— 賈瓦哈拉爾・尼赫魯（印度第一任總理，1889－1964）

Peace is not a relationship of nations. It is a condition of mind brought about by a serenity of soul. Peace is not merely the absence of war. It is also a state of mind. Lasting peace can come only to peaceful people.

—Jawaharlal Nehru

774

聖人被褐懷玉。

——老子（中國哲學家，約西元前七世紀－531 B.C.）

The sage wears rough clothing and holds the jewel in his heart.

—Lao-Tzu

775

得聞之樂音甜美，但那些未能得聞者，更為甜美。

—— 約翰·濟慈（英國詩人，1795-1821）

Heard melodies are sweet, but those unheard / Are sweeter . . .
—John Keats

776

生命中那些最動人的時刻，不總是在不語與靜謐之中嗎？

—— 馬歇·馬叟（法國戲劇家，1923-2007）

Do not the most moving moments of our lives find us all without words?
—Marcel Marceau

777

唯有向年輕人引介偉大的文學、戲劇與音樂，
以及那些振奮人心的科學發現，我們才能讓他
們體會到人類心靈中無限的可能性：他們也將
能夠懷抱夢想與前景。

—— 艾瑞克·安德森 (美國社會學家，1968-)

It is only by introducing the young to great literature, drama and
music, and to the excitement of great science that we open to them the
possibilities that lie within the human spirit—enable them to see visions
and dream dreams. —Eric Anderson

第五章
為政之道：政客抑或政治家？

CHAPTER 5
Politics and Politicians, Government and Statesmen

778

我們合眾國人民，為建立更完善的聯盟、樹立正義、保障國內安寧、提供共同防務、促進公共福利，並使我們自己和後代得享自由的幸福，特為美利堅合眾國制定本憲法。

——《美國憲法》

We the People of the United States, in order to form a more perfect union, establish justice, insure domestic tranquility, provide for the common defense, promote the general welfare, and secure the blessings of liberty to ourselves and our posterity, do ordain and establish this Constitution for the United States of America.

—The Constitution of the United States of America

779

我們認為下面這些真理是不言而喻的：造物者創造了平等的個人，並賦予他們若干不可剝奪的權利，其中包括生命權、自由權和追求幸福的權利。*

——《美國獨立宣言》

We hold these Truths to be self-evident, that all Men are created equal, that they are endowed by their Creator with certain unalienable Rights, that among these are Life, Liberty and the Pursuit of Happiness . . .

—Declaration of Independence

---

* 採用任東來在《美國憲政歷程：影響美國的25個司法大案》中的譯文（中國法制，2004）。

780

我對著上帝的祭壇發誓，將永遠地對抗奴役人類心靈的任何形式的暴政。

—— 湯瑪斯‧傑佛遜（美國第三任總統，1743-1826）

I have sworn upon the altar of God, eternal hostility against every form of tyranny over the mind of man.

—Thomas Jefferson

781

許多偉大的事物都是簡單的，且能夠以一個詞來表達：自由、正義、榮譽、責任、慈悲、希望。

—— 溫斯頓‧邱吉爾（前英國首相，1874-1965）

All the great things are simple, and many can be expressed in a single word: freedom; justice; honor; duty; mercy; hope.

—Sir Winston Churchill

782

一個為生命和自由作出最後犧牲的國家，將永不會被擊敗。

—— 穆斯塔法‧凱末爾‧阿塔圖克
（土耳其第一任總統，1881-1938）

A nation which makes the final sacrifice for life and freedom does not get beaten.

—Kemal Atatürk

783

唯有我們對於自由有著獨立信念，才能夠使我們保有自由。

—— 德懷特・艾森豪（美國第三十四任總統，1890-1969）

Only our individual faith in freedom can keep us free.

——Dwight D. Eisenhower

784

即使生命如此寶貴、和平如此甜美，但我們應當以鐵鍊與奴役做為代價嗎？全能的上帝呀，絕不！我不知道其他人會選擇何種道路，但是對我來說：不自由，毋寧死！

—— 派屈克・亨利（美國政治家、革命領導人，1736-1799）

Is life so dear, or peace so sweet, as to be purchased at the price of chains and slavery? Forbid it, Almighty God! I know not what course others may take; but as for me, give me liberty or give me death!

——Patrick Henry

785

那些期望採收自由的果實的人，必須要經歷足以支撐自由生活的勞苦。

—— 湯瑪斯·潘恩（英裔美國政治家、思想家，1737-1809）

Those who expect to reap the blessings of freedom must, like men, undergo the fatigue of supporting it.　　　　　—Thomas Paine

786

權力導致腐敗，而絕對的權力導致絕對的腐敗。

—— 約翰·達爾伯格·阿克頓男爵
（英國歷史學家，1834-1902）

Power tends to corrupt, and absolute power corrupts absolutely.
　　　　　　　　　　　　　　　　　　　　—Lord Acton

787

好的秩序是一切事物的基礎。

—— 埃德蒙·伯克
（英國政治家、哲學家、作家，1729-1797）

Good order is the foundation of all things.　　　　—Edmund Burke

788

請給我知的自由，以及以良心為本的言論自由。
這些高於其他一切形式的自由。

—— 約翰・米爾頓（英國詩人，1608-1674）

Give me the liberty to know, to utter, and to argue freely according to
my conscience, above all liberties. —John Milton

789

所有政治都關乎地方與基層。

—— 提普・歐尼爾（美國政治家，1912-1994）

All politics is local. —Thomas P. "Tip" O'Neil

790

那些寧願犧牲基本的自由來換取暫時性安全的
人，既不配擁有自由也不配擁有安全保障。

—— 班傑明・富蘭克林（美國政治家、作家，1706-1790）

They that can give up essential liberty to obtain a little temporary safety
deserve neither liberty nor safety. —Benjamin Franklin

791

一旦你放棄了人民對你的信心，就再也無法重拾他們對你的尊敬。你也許可以騙過所有人一次，或者每次都騙過某些人，但是你無法每次都騙過所有人。

—— 亞伯拉罕・林肯（美國第十六任總統，1809－1865）

If you once forfeit the confidence of your fellow citizens, you can never regain their respect and esteem. You may fool all of the people some of the time; you can even fool some of the people all of the time; but you can't fool all of the people all of the time.

—Abraham Lincoln

792

法律的語言，必須要是人民所能理解的。

—— 勒恩德・漢德（美國法官，1872－1961）

The language of the law must not be foreign to the ears of those who are to obey it.

—Learned Hand

793

那些被戰爭所征服、奴役的人，在失去自由之後，也會失去所有的美德。

—— 約翰·米爾頓（英國詩人，1608-1674）

The conquer'd, also, and enslaved by war, Shall, with their freedom lost, all virtue lose.　　　　　　　—John Milton

794

政治是一門找毛病的藝術：它探查毛病是否存在，然後錯誤地診斷、錯誤地治療。

—— 恩尼斯特·班恩（英國出版商，1875-1954）

Politics is the art of looking for trouble, finding it whether it exists or not, diagnosing it incorrectly, and applying the wrong remedy.

—Ernest Benn

795

政治選戰中最困難的，就是該如何避免顯露出你根本不配贏得勝利。

—— 阿德萊·E·史蒂文生（美國政治家，1900-1965）

The hardest thing about any political campaign is how to win without proving that you are unworthy of winning.

—Adlai E. Stevenson

796

倘若人民皆如綿羊般溫馴，就會塑造出如虎狼般的暴虐政府。

—— 伯川・德・朱馮內
（法國哲學家、政治經濟學家，1903–1987）

A society of sheep must in time beget a government of wolves.
—Bertrand de Jouvenel

797

自由就好似酒精一般：你淺嚐一口之後，就會上癮。

—— 法利・德昂（美國幽默作家，1867–1936）

Freedom is like drink. If you take any at all, you might as well take enough to make you happy for a while.
—Finley Peter Dunne

798

如果自由有任何意義，那就是在於告訴人民，他們有權利聽到所有他們不願聽到的事情。

—— 喬治・歐威爾（英國小說家、散文家，1903–1950）

If liberty means anything at all, it means the right to tell people what they do not want to hear.
—George Orwell

799

如果我們不相信言論自由能夠擴及到那些我們所鄙視之人，那我們其實對言論自由根本毫無信念可言。

——諾姆・杭士基（美國語言學家、哲學家，1928-）

If we do not believe in freedom of speech for those we despise we do not believe in it at all. ——Noam Chomsky

800

大部分的人並不想要自由，因為自由包括了責任。而大部分的人懼怕擔負責任。

——席格蒙・佛洛伊德（奧地利精神分析師，1856-1939）

Most people do not really want freedom, because freedom involves responsibility, and most people are frightened of responsibility.
——Sigmund Freud

801

在這個世界上，惟有維護他人的自由，才能保有自己的自由；我自由了，你也才能夠自由。

——克萊倫斯・達羅（美國律師，1857-1938）

You can only protect your liberties in this world by protecting the other man's freedom. You can only be free if I am free.
——Clarence Darrow

802

衡量一個人的方式，就是看他在掌握權力之後如何行事。

—— 庇塔庫斯（古希臘政治家，640–568 B.C.）

The measure of a man is what he does with power.

—Pittacus

803

邪惡之所以勝利，是因好人皆無為。

—— 埃德蒙·伯克
（英國政治家、哲學家、作家，1729–1797）

All that is necessary for the triumph of evil is that good men do nothing.

—Edmund Burke

804

真誠的外交，可以說是天方夜譚。

—— 約瑟夫·史達林（前蘇聯最高領導人，1878–1953）

A sincere diplomat is like dry water or wooden iron.

—Joseph Stalin

805

人類最傑出的時刻,就是在於他最自由的時刻。
如果我們能夠了解自由的原則,這道理就淺顯
易懂。我們必須記住,自由最基本的原則就是
選擇的自由。許多人都只是嘴上說說,但從未
將此原則放在心裡。

—— 但丁・阿利吉耶里(義大利詩人,1265-1321)

Mankind is at its best when it is most free. This will be clear if we grasp
the principle of liberty. We must recall that the basic principle of liberty
is freedom of choice, which saying many have on their lips but few in
their minds. —Dante Alighieri

806

互踢皮球,請到此為止。

—— 杜魯門(美國第三十三任總統,1884-1972)

The buck stops here. —Harry S. Truman

807

評價一位統治者的首要方法，就是看他如何用人。

——尼可洛·馬基維利
（義大利文藝復興政治家、作家，1469-1527）

The first method for estimating the intelligence of a ruler is to look at the men he has around him. ——Niccolò Machiavelli

808

政治的實際狀況就是：所有人都在忽視現實。

——亨利·布魯克斯·亞當斯
（美國歷史學家、作家，1838-1918）

Practical politics consists in ignoring facts.

——Henry Brooks Adams

809

真正的強者其實靜如處子。如果你需要告訴別人你的強大，那你其實根本不是真正的強者。

——瑪格麗特·柴契爾（前英國首相，1925-2013）

Being powerful is like being a lady. If you have to tell people you are— you aren't. ——Margaret Thatcher

810

在危機中的領導者總是能在潛意識作用下採取
適當的行動，而後才思及其行動的理由。

—— 賈瓦哈拉爾·尼赫魯（印度第一任總理，1889-1964）

A leader or a man of action in a crisis almost always acts subconsciously
and then thinks of the reasons for his action. —Jawaharlal Nehru

811

掌握當下的人就能掌握過去，而掌握過去的人
就能夠掌握未來。

—— 喬治·歐威爾（英國小說家、散文家，1903-1950）

Who controls the past controls the future. Who controls the present
controls the past. —George Orwell

812

抬頭挺胸地赴死，勝過奴顏屈膝地活著。

—— 艾米里亞諾·薩帕塔（墨西哥革命領袖，1879-1919）

It is better to die on your feet than to live on your knees.

—Emiliano Zapata

813

觀察敵人用什麼手段來嚇唬人，你就能發現他
們本身的恐懼所在。

—— 艾力‧賀佛爾（美國作家，1902-1983）

You can discover what your enemy fears most by observing the means
he uses to frighten you.
　　　　　　　　　　　　　　　　　　　　—Eric Hoffer

814

自由國家的真諦，就是將政府視為公眾的託付
與信賴。一切以國家為重，而非為了個人或政
黨的利益。

—— 約翰‧C‧卡爾宏（美國政治家，1782-1850）

The very essence of a free government consists in considering offices
as public trusts, bestowed for the good of the country, and not for the
benefit of an individual or a party.
　　　　　　　　　　　　　　　　　　　　—John C. Calhoun

815

這世界上最有價值的，是人類能夠自由探索的心靈。我願意捍衛的，是自由不羈的心靈；我堅決對抗的，是限制並毀滅心靈的任何思想、宗教和政府。

—— 約翰・史坦貝克（美國小說家，1902-1968）

The free, exploring mind of the individual human is the most valuable thing in the world. And this I would fight for: the freedom of the mind to take any direction it wishes, undirected. And this I must fight against: any idea, religion, or government which limits or destroys the individual.

—John Steinbeck

816

遲來的正義，等於是被否定的正義。

—— 知名法諺

Justice delayed is justice denied.

—Legal maxim

817

我只求自由。那些翩翩飛舞的蝴蝶都是自由的。

—— 查爾斯・狄更斯（英國小說家，1812-1870）

I only ask to be free. The butterflies are free.

—Charles Dickens

818

一個國家的真正偉大之處，在於那些形成偉大
人物的特質。

—— 查爾斯‧桑姆納（美國政治家，1811-1874）

The true greatness of nations is in those qualities which constitute the
greatness of the individual. —Charles Sumner

819

法治的最大用處，在於教導人民抗拒並棄絕暴
政與惡法。

—— 溫德爾‧菲利普斯（美國廢奴主義改革家，1811-1884）

The best use of laws is to teach men to trample bad laws under their
feet. —Wendell Phillips

820

政治並不是一門講求精確無誤的科學。

—— 奧托‧馮‧俾斯麥（德意志帝國宰相，1815-1890）

Politics is an inexact science. —Otto von Bismarck

821

所有人不分男女皆是生來平等。此為無需證明的事實。

—— 伊麗莎白·卡迪·斯坦頓
（美國社會改革家、婦女參政運動者，1815-1902）

We hold these truths to be self-evident, that all men and women are created equal. —Elizabeth Cady Stanton

822

無代表，不納稅。

—— 美國獨立革命口號

No taxation without representation.
—Rallying cry of the American Revolution

823

沒有人能夠凌駕於法律之上。當我們要求一個人遵守法律時，並不需要徵求他的同意。守法是義務，並非是賣好的人情。

—— 西奧多·羅斯福（美國第二十六任總統，1858-1919）

No man is above the law and no man is below it; nor do we ask any man's permission when we require him to obey it. Obedience of the law is demanded; not asked as a favor. —Theodore Roosevelt

824

我必須鑽研政治與戰爭之道，我的孩子才能夠有鑽研數學與哲學的自由。

—— 約翰・亞當斯（美國第二任總統，1735-1826）

I must study politics and war that my sons may have liberty to study mathematics and philosophy.

—John Adams

825

一個看重特權更甚於原則的民族，很快地會失去這兩者。

—— 德懷特・艾森豪（美國第三十四任總統，1890-1969）

A people that values its privileges above its principles soon loses both.

—Dwight D. Eisenhower

826

你有權利讓別人聽見你的聲音，但你未必有權利要求別人正視你的意見。

—— 休伯特・韓福瑞（美國第三十八任副總統，1911-1978）

The right to be heard does not automatically include the right to be taken seriously.

—Hubert H. Humphrey

827

民主的死亡，不會是由某個暴力行動所造成的突發事件。而是由無情、冷漠以及失調所造成的慢性毀滅。

—— 羅伯特‧梅伊納德‧哈欽斯
（美國教育哲學家，1899-1977）

The death of democracy is not likely to be an assassination from ambush. It will be a slow extinction from apathy, indifference, and undernourishment.
—Robert Hutchins

828

當人變成了只會算計的動物，這是全人類文明的退步，而戰爭只是其表徵。

—— 約翰‧史坦貝克（美國小說家，1902-1968）

All war is a symptom of man's failure as a thinking animal.
—John Steinbeck

829

我並非憤世嫉俗。我只是喜愛常識、誠實和端
正的品性。而這些特質使我遠離官場。

——H·L·孟肯（美國編輯、評論家，1880-1956）

It is inaccurate to say I hate everything. I am strongly in favor of
common sense, common honesty, and common decency. This makes me
forever ineligible for any public office.　　　　—H. L. Mencken

830

如果世界上有許多地方容不下以良心為本的自
由思想和個人判斷，就讓那些受難者們都來美
國吧。讓我們珍惜這些高貴的客人，並且以永
恆寬容的羽翼庇護他們。

——塞繆爾·亞當斯（美國革命家、政治家，1722-1803）

Freedom of thought and the right to private judgment, in matters of
conscience, driven from every corner of the earth, direct their course to
this happy country as their last asylum. Let us cherish the noble guests,
and shelter them under the wings of universal toleration.

　　　　　　　　　　　　　　　　　　—Samuel Adams

831

世上很少有事物是全然邪惡或全然善良的。幾乎所有事情，尤其是政府的政策，都不可避免地結合了兩者。所以從政者總是需要能夠事前深思熟慮，衡量兩者的輕重。

—— 亞伯拉罕·林肯（美國第十六任總統，1809-1865）

There are few things wholly evil or wholly good. Almost everything, especially of government policy, is an inseparable compound of the two, so that our best judgment of the preponderance between them is continually demanded. —Abraham Lincoln

832

那些腐化大眾心靈的人，就如同國庫的竊賊一般邪惡。

—— 阿德萊·E·史蒂文生（美國政治家，1900-1965）

Those who corrupt the public mind are just as evil as those who steal from the public purse. —Adlai E. Stevenson

833

一個人的雙足可停駐於祖國，但他的雙眼應當
審視全世界。

—— 喬治・桑塔亞那（美國哲學家、詩人，1863－1952）

A man's feet should be planted in his country, but his eyes should survey
the world.

—George Santayana

834

在政治界，愚蠢並非是一種障礙。

—— 拿破崙・波拿巴（法國皇帝、軍事家，1769－1821）

In politics stupidity is not a handicap.

—Napoléon Bonaparte

835

人生之中，除了死亡和納稅之外，沒有什麼是
真實的。

—— 班傑明・富蘭克林（美國政治家、作家，1706－1790）

Nothing in life is certain except death and taxes.

—Benjamin Franklin

836

我揭露了這個國家的奴隸制度，因為揭露它即是消滅它。奴役就好似黑暗中的怪物，真理的光亮就是它的死亡。

—— 菲德利克・道格拉斯
（美國廢奴主義作家、演說家，1818-1895）

I expose slavery in this country, because to expose it is to kill it. Slavery is one of those monsters of darkness to whom the light of truth is death.

—Frederick Douglass

837

一個真正的共和國，代表的就是每個人的權利，不分男女。

—— 法蘭克林・亞當斯（美國專欄作家，1881-1960）

The true republic: men, their rights and nothing more; women, their rights and nothing less.

—Franklin P. Adams

838

我不知道人們會用什麼樣的武器來打第三次世界大戰。我知道的是，第四次世界大戰將是場棍棒與石塊的戰爭。

—— 愛因斯坦（猶太裔美國物理學家，1879-1955）

I know not with what weapons World War III will be fought, but World War IV will be fought with sticks and stones. —Albert Einstein

839

宇宙或許有其極限，但人的愚蠢絕對沒有極限。

—— 愛因斯坦（猶太裔美國物理學家，1879-1955）

Two things are infinite: the universe and human stupidity; and I'm not sure about the universe. —Albert Einstein

840

就算是成文的法律，也不是永遠都不能修改的。

—— 亞里斯多德（希臘哲學家，384-322 B.C.）

Even when laws have been written down, they ought not always to remain unaltered. —Aristotle

841

寬容所造成的，不是大好，就是大惡。

—— 埃德蒙・伯克
（英國政治家、哲學家、作家，1729-1797）

Toleration is good for all, or it is good for none.

—Edmund Burke

842

人類歷史的進展，告訴了我們，人類的自由與權利，都是來自於真誠熱切的奮鬥。如果沒有奮鬥，就不會有進步。那些聲稱支持自由，卻反對激進行動的人，就好似不願犁田卻期待收成、渴望甘霖卻厭惡雷聲、想親近海洋卻又害怕浪濤之人。

—— 菲德利克・道格拉斯
（美國廢奴主義作家、演說家，1818-1895）

The whole history of the progress of human liberty shows that all concessions yet made to her august claims have been born of earnest struggle. . . . If there is no struggle, there is no progress. Those who profess to favor freedom, and yet deprecate agitation, are men who want crops without plowing up the ground, they want rain without thunder and lightning. They want the ocean without the awful roar of its many waters.

—Frederick Douglass

843

在一個全民皆盲的國度，獨眼之人就能稱王。

—— 德希德里烏斯·伊拉斯謨
（尼德蘭哲學家、神學家，1466 - 1536）

In the country of the blind the one-eyed man is king.

—Deciderius Erasmus

844

我們的法律一視同仁，同時禁止富人和窮人露宿街頭、行乞和偷竊。

—— 安那托爾·佛朗士（法國作家，1844 - 1924）

The Law, in its majestic equality, forbids the rich, as well as the poor, to sleep under the bridges, to beg in the streets, and to steal bread.

—Anatole France

845

那些只想著維護自己的名譽和社會地位的謹慎
之人，永遠都無法實行改革。那些真心要實行
改革的人，是願意付出一切甚至失去一切的。
無論於公於私，無論合宜與否，他們都同情那
些受壓迫的思想和弱者，並且肩負起一切後果。

—— 蘇珊‧B‧安東尼（美國婦女參政運動者，1820-1906）

Cautious, careful people always casting about to preserve their reputation
or social standards never can bring about reform. Those who are really in
earnest are willing to be anything or nothing in the world's estimation,
and publicly and privately, in season and out, avow their sympathies
with despised ideas and their advocates, and bear the consequences.

—Susan B. Anthony

846

一個有勇氣的人，能夠與千軍萬馬抗衡。

—— 湯瑪斯‧傑佛遜（美國第三任總統，1743-1826）

One man with courage is a majority. —Thomas Jefferson

847

任何一個地方所發生的不公不義，都是對所有地方公義的威脅。

—— 馬丁·路德·金恩
（美國牧師、非裔美國人權運動領袖，1929–1968）

Injustice anywhere is a threat to justice everywhere.

—Martin Luther King, Jr.

848

讓我將今日的訊息超越時間與空間，傳遞給我們的盟友，也傳遞給我們的敵人：新一世代的美國人民已經接下了火炬。他們生於本世紀，受過戰爭的磨練，也受到艱苦贏得的和平的陶冶，並以先人的傳統為傲。他們絕不願目睹或允許人權逐步受到侵害，因為人權乃是這個國家致力去維護的，無論是在國內或是在世界的任何一個地方。

讓每一個國家無論敵我，都能清楚地了解：我們願意付出任何代價，承擔任何責任，面對任何困難，支持任何一位盟友，對抗任何敵人，來確保民主自由的存在與茁壯。

讓我們重新開始，謹記謙恭有禮並非是虛弱的徵象，而誠意則永遠受到實證的考驗。讓我們並非因恐懼而談判，但也讓我們永遠無懼於談判。

這些種種工作，不能夠在一百天內完成，也不能夠在一千天內完成，或許也無法在我的任期內完成，甚至不能在我們存在於地球上的時日內完成，但是就讓我們有個開始吧！

所以，我的美國同胞們：不要問你們的國家能夠為你們做什麼，要問問你們自己，能夠為這個國家付出什麼。

——約翰・F・甘迺迪（美國第三十五任總統，1917－1963）

Let the word go forth from this time and place, to friend and foe alike, that the torch has been passed to a new generation of Americans—born in this century, tempered by war, disciplined by a hard and bitter peace, proud of our ancient heritage—and unwilling to witness or permit the slow undoing of those human rights to which this Nation has always been committed, and to which we are committed today at home and around the world.

Let every nation know, whether it wishes us well or ill, that we shall pay any price, bear any burden, meet any hardship, support any friend, oppose any foe, in order to assure the survival and the success of liberty.

So let us begin anew—remembering on both sides that civility is not a sign of weakness, and sincerity is always subject to proof. Let us never negotiate out of fear. But let us never fear to negotiate.

All this will not be finished in the first 100 days. Nor will it be finished in the first 1,000 days, nor in the life of this Administration, nor even perhaps in our lifetime on this planet. But let us begin.

And so, my fellow Americans: ask not what your country can do for you—ask what you can do for your country.

—John F. Kennedy

849

即使在世界上的所有人之中，只有一個人有不同的意見，其他人也沒有理由不讓他表達意見。就像如果這個人掌握了權力，其他人也沒有理由都保持沈默。

——約翰·史都華·彌爾
（英國哲學家、政治經濟學家，1806-1873）

If mankind minus one were of one opinion, then mankind is no more justified in silencing the one than the one—if he had the power—would be justified in silencing mankind.
——John Stuart Mill

850

政客都精通「模糊」的藝術。他們的話語總是迂迴且圓滑，因為他們知道如果言詞犀利如鋒，隨時都可能會傷到自己。

——愛德華·R·默羅（美國媒體工作者，1908-1965）

The politician is . . . trained in the art of inexactitude. His words tend to be blunt or rounded, because if they have a cutting edge they may later return to wound him.
——Edward R. Murrow

851

差勁的官員就是由那些放棄投票權的好公民所
拱上位的。

—— 喬治‧吉恩‧內森（美國劇場評論家，1882-1985）

Bad officials are elected by good citizens who do not vote.

—George Jean Nathan

852

只有那些從未經歷過戰爭之人，才會將戰爭視
為有趣的事。

—— 德希德里烏斯‧伊拉斯謨
（尼德蘭哲學家、神學家，1466-1536）

War is delightful to those who have had no experience of it.

—Desiderius Erasmus

853

避戰和備戰，無法同時進行。

—— 愛因斯坦（猶太裔美國物理學家，1879-1955）

You cannot simultaneously prevent and prepare for war.

—Albert Einstein

854

人類有實行正義的能力，這讓民主成為可能；
但人性也易使人忽視正義，這使民主成為必需。

—— 雷因霍爾德·尼布爾（美國神學家，1892-1971）

Man's capacity for justice makes democracy possible; but man's
inclination to injustice makes democracy necessary.

—Reinhold Niebuhr

855

英語之中，最令人害怕的一句話就是：「我是
政府單位的人，我想您需要我的幫助」。

—— 隆納·雷根（美國第四十任總統，1911-2004）

The nine most terrifying words in the English language are, "I'm from
the government and I'm here to help."　　　　—Ronald Reagan

856

法律並不會說服你遵守它，而是威脅你遵守它。

—— 大塞內加（古羅馬修辭學家、作家，54 B.C.-39 A.D.）

Laws do not persuade just because they threaten.　　　—Seneca

857

如果怕熱就別進廚房。

—— 杜魯門（美國第三十三任總統，1884-1972）

If you can't stand the heat, get out of the kitchen.

—Harry S. Truman

858

政客都是一個樣地亂開支票：明明這兒沒有任何河流，卻說要建造橋樑。

—— 尼基塔·赫魯雪夫（前蘇聯總理，1894-1971）

Politicians are the same all over. They promise to build bridges even when there are no rivers.

—Nikita Khruschev

859

一個人冷靜的判斷可抵過好幾個急匆匆結束的會議。我們需要的是理性的光亮，而非激情的火焰。

—— 伍德羅·威爾遜（美國第二十八任總統，1856-1924）

One cool judgment is worth a dozen hasty councils. The thing to do is to supply light and not heat.

—Woodrow Wilson

860

對抗暴政即是服從上帝。

—— 湯瑪斯·傑佛遜（美國第三任總統，1743-1826）

Rebellion to tyrants is obedience to God.　　　　—Thomas Jefferson

861

如果窮人的悲慘並非是自然天擇的結果，而是
人為制度造成的，那我們可說是罪孽深重。

—— 查爾斯·達爾文
（美國自然學家、進化論者，1809-1882）

If the misery of the poor be caused not by the laws of nature, but by our
institutions, great is our sin.　　　　—Charles Darwin

862

法律即為秩序；良善的法律意味著好的秩序。

—— 亞里斯多德（希臘哲學家，384-322 B. C.）

Law is order, and good law is good order.　　　　—Aristotle

863

人生來自由，但卻處處困於枷鎖之中。當一個人認為自己主宰了別人時，其實他自己的奴性比誰都堅強。

—— 尚・雅克・盧梭 (法國哲學家，1712-1778)

Man is born free; and everywhere he is in chains. One thinks himself the master of others, and still remains a greater slave than they.

—Jean-Jacques Rousseau

864

自由也包括了保持緘默的權利。

—— 1968年法國學生運動標語

Liberty is the right to silence.

—Graffiti during French student riots, 1968

865

在某些情況下，非暴力抗爭需要比暴力抗爭更強悍的戰鬥精神。

—— 凱薩・查維斯
(美國勞工領袖、民權運動人士，1927-1993)

In some cases non-violence requires more militancy than violence.

—César Chávez

866

一個人打從心裡相信的事，即便不是真實的，
也將會成為真實。

—— 約翰·李利（英國作家，1553–1606）

In the province of the mind, what one believes to be true either is true or becomes true.
　　　　　　　　　　　　　　　　　　　　　—John Lilly

867

自由並非是我們生來就擁有的；我們必須為自
由奮鬥，並且在每個世代都守護它。因為對一
個民族來說，自由的機會只有一次。那些曾經
享有自由然後失去自由的人們，將再也無法重
獲自由。

—— 隆納·雷根（美國第四十任總統，1911–2004）

Freedom . . . is not ours by inheritance; it must be fought for and defended constantly by each generation, for it comes only once to a people. Those who have known freedom, and then lost it, have never known it again.
　　　　　　　　　　　　　　　　　　　　—Ronald Reagan

868

在我們希望能確保安全的未來中，我們期待建立一個以四大基本自由為根基的世界。首先是普世的言論自由。第二，則是普世的宗教自由。第三，是免於匱乏的自由，也就是每個國家必須要具備基礎的經濟知識，確保其國民享有健康的和平生活。最後，是免於恐懼的自由，這意味著全球規模的裁減軍備，使每一個國家都無法對鄰近的他國進行任何武裝的敵對行動。而這同樣也必須是普及全世界的自由。

——富蘭克林·D·羅斯福
（美國第三十二任總統，1882-1945）

The future days, which we seek to make secure, we look forward to a world founded upon four essential human freedoms. The first is freedom of speech and expression—everywhere in the world. The second is freedom of every person to worship God in his own way—everywhere in the world. The third is freedom from want— which, translated into world terms, means economic understandings which will secure to every nation a healthy peacetime life for its inhabitants—everywhere in the world. The fourth is freedom from fear—which, translated into world terms, means a world-wide reduction of armaments to such a point and in such a thorough fashion that no nation will be in a position to commit an act of physical aggression against any neighbor—anywhere in the world.
　　　　　　　　　　　　　　　　　　—Franklin Delano Roosevelt

869

在戰爭期間，媒體自由是尤為重要的。

—— 威廉·布拉（美國政治家，1865-1940）

Of all times in time of war the press should be free.

—William Borah

870

對自由的最大威脅，是那些鄉愿之人。他們雖然熱情善良，但卻無法全面理解自由的真諦，他們是潛在的禍害。

—— 路易·D·布雷迪斯（美國最高法院法官，1856-1941）

The greatest dangers to liberty lurk in insidious encroachment by men of zeal, well-meaning, but without understanding.

—Louis D. Brandeis

871

剝奪一個人的發言權利，並不代表你就說服了他。

—— 約翰·莫里子爵（英國政治家，1838-1923）

You have not converted a man because you have silenced him.

—Viscount John Morley

872

我和那些倖存下來的少數人一樣了解戰爭，而
再也沒有什麼能夠比戰爭更令人感到厭惡的事
了。我長久以來一直支持完全廢止戰爭。即便
不論對敵我雙方的毀滅性，戰爭絕非是處理國
際爭端的有效辦法。

—— 道格拉斯・麥克阿瑟（美國將軍，1880－1964）

I know war as few men now living know it, and nothing to me is more
revolting. I have long advocated its complete abolition, as its very
destructiveness on both friend and foe has rendered it useless as a means
of settling international disputes.

—General Douglas MacArthur

873

如果任何一個國家不重視自由，她終將失去自
由。而諷刺的是，如果她重視的是安逸與財富，
她也註定會失去安逸與財富。

—— 威廉・薩默塞特・毛姆
（英國小說家、劇作家，1874－1965）

If a nation values anything more than freedom, it will lose its freedom;
and the irony of it is that if it is comfort or money that it values more, it
will lose that too.　　　　　　　　　　　　—W. Somerset Maugham

874

如果所謂的自由並不包括犯錯的自由，那這樣的自由並不值得擁有。我無法理解那些已經具備經驗和能力的人，居然能夠隨意地剝奪別人這一項珍貴的權利。

—— 甘地（印度民族主義領袖，1869-1948）

Freedom is not worth having if it does not connote freedom to err. It passes my comprehension how human beings, be they ever so experienced and able, can delight in depriving other human beings of that precious right. —Mohandas Gandhi

875

那些不屑參與政治的聰明人所受到的懲罰，就是被糟糕的人統治。

—— 柏拉圖（希臘哲學家，427-347 B.C.）

The punishment which the wise suffer who refuse to take part in the government, is to live under the government of worse men.

—Plato

876

那些放棄社會改革使命之人，就如同放棄了作為自由人的責任。

—— 艾倫·帕頓（南非作家，1903－1988）

To give up the task of reforming society is to give up one's responsibility as a free man. —Alan Paton

877

我們從歷史中學到的教訓，就是我們從來沒有從歷史中學到教訓。

—— 格奧爾格·威廉·弗里德里希·黑格爾
（德國哲學家，1770－1831）

We learn from history that we do not learn from history. —Georg Wilhelm Friedrich Hegel

878

人們也許不靠話語過活，但是有時他們得吞下自己說過的話。

—— 阿德萊·E·史蒂文生（美國政治家，1900－1965）

Man does not live by words alone, despite the fact that sometimes he has to eat them. —Adlai E. Stevenson

879

打擊邪惡最有效的方式，就是將它攤在陽光下，
讓大眾恥笑。人可以對抗駁斥，但是無法忍受
譏嘲：邪惡之人對於為惡已有心理準備，但是
他痛恨暴露出自身的荒謬。

—— 莫里哀（法國劇作家，1622-1673）

The most effective way of attacking vice is to expose it to public ridicule.
People can put up with rebukes, but they cannot bear being laughed at:
they are prepared to be wicked but they dislike appearing ridiculous.

—Molière

880

所謂自由，就是掌握自己人生發展的能力，也
就是形塑自我的能力。

—— 羅洛・梅（美國心理學家，1909-1994）

Freedom is man's capacity to take a hand in his own development. It is
our capacity to mold ourselves.　　　　　—Rollo May

881

當人類能夠隨心所欲時，他們通常會互相模仿。

—— 艾力・賀佛爾（美國作家，1902-1983）

When people are free to do as they please, they usually imitate each
other.　　　　　—Eric Hoffer

882

縱然是千萬人眾口一詞，也不能為謬誤之事背書。

—— 奧利弗・戈德史密斯（愛爾蘭詩人、作家，1728-1774）

The united voice of millions cannot lend the smallest foundation to falsehood. —Oliver Goldsmith

883

如果你是對的，你再怎樣激進都不為過；如果你是錯的，你再怎麼保守都不夠。

—— 馬丁・路德・金恩
（美國牧師、非裔美國人權運動領袖，1929-1968）

When you are right, you cannot be too radical; When you are wrong, you cannot be too conservative. —Martin Luther King, Jr.

884

「異端邪說」乃是自由思想的同義字。

—— 葛蘭姆・葛林（英國小說家、劇作家，1904-1991）

Heresy is another word for freedom of thought.

—Graham Greene

885

一個能讓人民予取予求的政府，也能夠輕易地奪走人民的一切事物。

—— 巴瑞・戈德瓦特（美國政治家，1909-1998）

A government that is big enough to give you all you want is big enough to take it all away. —Barry Goldwater

886

一個偷馬賊被絞死，並非是作為其偷馬的懲罰，而是作為一種警告，用以嚇阻其他人偷竊馬匹。

—— 喬治・塞維爾，哈利福克斯侯爵（英國政治家、作家，1633-1695）

Men are not hanged for stealing horses, but that horses may not be stolen. —George Savile, Marquess of Halifax

887

美國政治體系的基礎，就在於人民擁有能夠主導政府的權利。

—— 喬治・華盛頓（美國第一任總統，1732-1799）

The basis of our political system is the right of the people to make and to alter their constitutions of government.

—George Washington

888

心靈的自由，不只需要擺脫律法的約束，更要納入另類的思考。最成功的專制，並非是運用武力來維持一致性，而是消滅人民對於其他可能性的意識。

—— 艾倫‧布魯（美國社會學家、作家，1930-1992）

Freedom of the mind requires not only, or not even specially, the absence of legal constraints but the presence of alternative thoughts. The most successful tyranny is not the one that uses force to assure uniformity but the one that removes the awareness of other possibilities.

—Alan Bloom

889

地獄中烈焰最為熾熱的地方，是留給那些在重大道德危機中仍保持中立的人。

—— 但丁‧阿利吉耶里（義大利詩人，1265-1321）

The hottest places in hell are reserved for those who in times of great moral crises maintain their neutrality.

—Dante Alighieri

890

美國絕不會被外敵所擊敗。如果我們遭受挫敗、喪失自由，必然是來自於自我毀滅。

——亞伯拉罕·林肯（美國第十六任總統，1809-1865）

America will never be destroyed from the outside. If we falter and lose our freedoms, it will be because we destroyed ourselves.

——Abraham Lincoln

891

我恨拙劣，就如同我痛恨罪惡，而我尤其痛恨政治上的拙劣，因為那會毀掉千千萬萬人的人生。

——歌德（德國戲劇家、詩人，1749-1832）

I hate all bungling as I do sin, but particularly bungling in politics, which leads to the misery and ruin of many thousands and millions of people.

——Johann Wolfgang von Goethe

第六章

諺語的智慧

CHAPTER 6

Proverbial Wisdom

892

我們可以藉由諺語的品質來評價一個國家。

——德國諺語

A country can be judged by the quality of its proverbs.

—German proverb

893

些許的耐心勝過大智大慧。

——荷蘭諺語

A handful of patience is worth more than a bushel of brains.

—Dutch proverb

894

對於得不到的東西，人們通常用鄙視來遮掩自己的失落。

——伊索寓言〈狐狸與葡萄〉

It is easy to despise what you cannot get.

—*Aesop*, "The Fox and the Grapes"

895

一個懂得閉上嘴巴的傻瓜，其實不算是真的傻。
—— 意第緒諺語

A quiet fool is half a sage.　　　　　　　　　—Yiddish proverb

896

雙鳥在林不如一鳥在手。
—— 英文諺語

A bird in the hand is worth two in the bush.　　　　—English proverb

897

今日的節儉，是為了明日的匱乏做準備。
—— 伊索寓言〈螞蟻與蟋蟀〉

It is thrifty to prepare today for the wants of tomorrow.
—*Aesop*, "The Ant and the Grasshopper"

898

團結就是力量。

——伊索寓言〈一綑樹枝〉

Union gives strength.　　　　　　　——*Aesop*, "The Bundle of Sticks"

899

如果你想讓上帝發笑，就告訴他你那「萬全」的計畫吧。

——意第緒諺語

If you want to give God a good laugh, tell Him your plans.
　　　　　　　　——Yiddish proverb

900

討好所有人，就等於得罪所有人。

——伊索寓言〈人、男孩與驢子〉

Please all, and you will please none.
　　　　　——*Aesop*, "The Man, the Boy, and the Donkey"

901

既然房子都著火了，我們乾脆就以它取暖吧。

—— 義大利諺語

Since the house is on fire, let us warm ourselves.

—Italian proverb

902

人們總是為了自己得不到事物而對他人懷恨在心。

—— 伊索寓言〈馬槽中的狗〉

People often grudge others what they cannot enjoy themselves.

—*Aesop*, "The Dog in the Manger"

903

我們總是給予敵人能夠毀滅我們自己的工具。

—— 伊索寓言〈鷹與箭〉

We often give our enemies the means of our own destruction.

—*Aesop*, "The Eagle and the Arrow"

904

身處在安全的距離之外時，要展現勇氣是很容易的。

——伊索寓言〈野狼與小孩〉

It is easy to be brave from a safe distance.

—*Aesop*, "The Wolf and the Kid"

905

平靜的水面之下，也可能潛藏著鱷魚。

——馬來諺語

Don't think there are no crocodiles because the water is calm.

—Malayan proverb

906

雞蛋還未孵出前，別急著計算小雞的數量。

——伊索寓言〈擠奶女工和她的桶子〉

Do not count your chickens before they are hatched.

—*Aesop*, "The Milk Woman and Her Pail"

907

千里之行，始於足下。

——中國諺語

A journey of a thousand miles begins with a single step.

—Chinese proverb

908

一群由獅子所領導的綿羊，能夠擊敗一群由綿羊所領導的獅子。

——阿拉伯諺語

An army of sheep led by a lion would defeat an army of lions led by a sheep.

—Arabic proverb

909

拖延乃是時間的竊賊。

——世界諺語

Procrastination is the thief of time.

—Proverb found in many cultures

910

切莫為了追求虛無的影子，而錯失了實在的事物。

—— 伊索寓言〈狗與影子〉

Beware lest you lose the substance by grasping at the shadow.
—*Aesop*, "The Dog and the Shadow"

911

若真心疼愛你的孩子，就讓他出門遠行吧。

—— 日本諺語

If you love your children, send them out into the world.
—Japanese proverb

912

最好的鎧甲，就是保持安全的距離。

—— 義大利諺語

The best armor is to keep out of range.
—Italian proverb

913

人總是對模仿者刮目相看，並輕視了真正的事物。

—— 伊索寓言〈小丑與鄉下人〉

Men often applaud an imitation, and hiss the real thing.
—*Aesop*, "The Buffoon and the Countryman"

914

滴水穿石。

—— 中國諺語

Dripping water pierces a stone.　—Chinese proverb

915

倘若蜘蛛們同心協力，牠們亦有能耐網羅住一隻猛獅。

—— 衣索比亞諺語

When spiders unite, they can tie down a lion.
—Ethiopian proverb

916

當友情升溫至燃點，就會冒出愛情的火花。

—— 法國諺語

Love is friendship set on fire.

—French proverb

917

失去一位朋友，就好似斷了一隻手臂。

—— 德國諺語

The death of a friend is equivalent to the loss of a limb.

—German proverb

918

你要縱情歌唱跳舞，彷彿全世界都觀賞著一樣。
用心地活著，將每一天都當作是你生命中的最
後一天。

—— 愛爾蘭諺語

Dance as if no one's watching, sing as if no one's listening, and live everyday as if it were your last.

—Irish proverb

919

所有事物有都其隱而不現的面向，而其中又必然有更深層的面向。

—— 日本諺語

The reverse side also has a reverse side. —Japanese proverb

920

棋局結束之後，無論是國王或士卒，都會回到同一個盒子裡。

—— 義大利諺語

At the end of the game, the king and the pawn go back in the same box. —Italian proverb

921

越老的琴弦，能奏出越甜美的音樂。

—— 愛爾蘭諺語

The older the fiddle, the sweeter the tune. —Irish proverb

922

光有願景而無行動，不過是白日夢罷了。而沒有願景的行動，則會造成恐怖的噩夢。

——世界諺語

Vision without action is daydream. Action without vision is nightmare.

——Proverb found in many cultures

923

氣量與勇氣兼具的人，就能擁有最美好的人生。

——挪威諺語

The generous and bold have the best lives.

——Norwegian proverb

924

一個人恐懼的深淺，端看於他心靈的強弱。

——日本諺語

Fear is only as deep as the mind allows.

——Japanese proverb

925

勇於面對光明，黑影自然會落在你的身後。

—— 紐西蘭毛利族諺語

Turn your face to the sun and the shadows fall behind you.

—Maori proverb

926

塞翁失馬，焉知非福。

—— 中國諺語

The future is always unpredictable; the trouble you face can be a bless in disguise.

—Chinese proverb

927

寧做一日之雄獅，也不願身為羔羊度過千日。

—— 羅馬諺語

It is better to live one day as a lion, than a thousand days as a lamb.

—Roman proverb

928

教堂已經關閉，道路也已經結霜。酒館路途遙遠，但我會緩步慢行。

—— 俄羅斯諺語

The church is close, but the road is icey. The tavern is far, but I will walk carefully.
—Russian proverb

929

死水不深。

—— 薩米人諺語

Water that does not move, is always shallow.
—Sami proverb

930

那些不以慷慨待人，不懂享受生活情趣之人，就好像鐵匠庸庸碌碌地吹喝著，雖然呼嘯著氣息，卻從未真正地活著。

—— 梵文諺語

He who allows his day to pass by without practicing generosity and enjoying life's pleasures is like a blacksmith's bellows—he breathes but does not live.
—Sanskrit proverb

931

以謙遜持身，因為人人皆為塵泥所塑。以高貴待人，因為人人皆為繁星降世。

—— 塞爾維亞諺語

Be humble for you are made of earth. Be noble for you are made of stars.
—Serbian proverb

932

撫養一個孩子長大成人，需要傾注全村之力。

—— 非洲諺語

It takes an entire village to raise a child
—African proverb

933

少些恐懼，多些希望；少些吞嚥，多些咀嚼；少些抱怨，多些呼吸；少些閒話，多些交流；少些憎恨，多些關愛。如此，你將擁有所有美好的事物。

—— 瑞典諺語

Fear less, hope more; eat less, chew more; whine less, breathe more; talk less, say more; hate less, love more; and all good things are yours.
—Swedish proverb

934

堅忍者雖然步伐緩慢，仍將贏得勝利。

—— 伊索寓言〈龜兔賽跑〉

Slow and steady wins the race.

—*Aesop*, "The Tortoise and the Hare"

935

向不可能之處追尋，以探求最大的可能性。

—— 義大利諺語

By asking for the impossible, obtain the best possible.

—Italian proverb

936

抬頭向神祈禱的同時，也要不時低頭注意，讓船避開礁石。

—— 印度諺語

Call on God, but row away from the rocks.　　　—Indian proverb

937

三十六計，走為上策。

—— 中國諺語

The smartest thing in a tight situation is to beat a retreat.

—Chinese proverb

938

就算是一個壞掉的時鐘，一天之中也會有兩個時刻是正確的。

—— 波蘭諺語

Even a clock that does not work is right twice a day.

—Polish proverb

939

緊行無好步。

—— 台灣諺語

He who hurries can not walk with dignity.　—Taiwanese proverb

940

在知道新的水桶不會漏水前，可先別把舊的水桶扔了。

——瑞典諺語

Don't throw away the old bucket until you know whether the new one holds water.　　　　　　—Swedish proverb

941

這是壓倒駱駝的最後一根稻草。

——英文諺語

It's the final straw that broke the camel's back.

—English proverb

942

告訴我一件事，我可能會忘記；展現給我看，我也可能無法記得；讓我也加入其中，我才能夠真正理解。

——美洲原住民諺語

Tell me and I'll forget. Show me, and I may not remember. Involve me, and I'll understand.　　　　　　—Native American proverb

943

對雌鵝好的，對雄鵝也自然是好的。

—— 英文諺語

What's good for the goose is good for the gander.

—English proverb

944

成日與鼠輩為伍，自然滿身跳蚤。

—— 英文諺語

He who lies down with dogs, rises with fleas.

—English proverb

945

一個從未得到偷竊機會的人，未必就是真正誠實的人。

—— 俄羅斯諺語

A man is not honest simply because he never had a chance to steal.

—Russian proverb

946

一個酒店老闆愛死酒鬼了，但他可不想自己的
女婿是個這樣的人。

—— 意第緒諺語

The innkeeper loves the drunkard, but not for a son-in-law.
—Yiddish proverb

947

逝去的時間和說出口的話都無法收回，縱使只
是發生在昨日。

—— 愛沙尼亞諺語

Time and words can't be recalled, even if it was only yesterday.
—Estonian proverb

948

揠苗助長。

—— 中國諺語

You won't help shoots grow by pulling them up higher.
—Chinese proverb

949

對著壞天氣咒罵，並無助於耕作。

—— 英文諺語

Cursing the weather is never good farming.　　　—English proverb

950

太多的廚師反而會搞砸一鍋湯：人多手雜。

—— 英文諺語

Too many cooks spoil the broth.　　　—English proverb

951

求教於有學問的人，不如求教於有經驗的人。

—— 阿拉伯諺語

Ask the experienced rather than the learned.　　　—Arabic proverb

952
莫浪費，莫貪求。

—— 世界諺語

Waste not, want not.　　　　　　　　—Proverb found in many cultures

953
「明天」總會是一年中最忙碌的一天。

—— 西班牙諺語

Tomorrow is often the busiest time of the year.

—Spanish proverb

954
過度的休息使人生鏽。

—— 德國諺語

When I rest, I rust.　　　　　　　　　—German proverb

955

復仇是一道等越久越美味的佳餚。

—— 義大利諺語

Revenge is a dish best served cold.

—Italian proverb

956

走出自家的大門，你就已經踏出了旅程中最艱難的一步。

—— 法蘭德斯諺語

He who is outside his door has the hardest part of his journey behind him.

—Flemish proverb

957

沒有人會認為自己的情人是醜陋的。

—— 丹麥諺語

Nobody's sweetheart is ugly.

—Dutch proverb

958

冬天時馬車閒置，夏天時雪橇也偷懶著。只有馬兒全年無休。

—— 意第緒諺語

The wagon rests in winter, the sleigh in summer, the horse never.

—Yiddish proverb

959

同樣羽毛的鳥兒成群結隊：物以類聚。

—— 英文諺語

Birds of a feather flock together.

—English proverb

960

把馬匹借給別人去遠行，到時候你恐怕只能要回一張馬皮。

—— 英文諺語

Lend a horse, and you may have back his skin.

—English proverb

961

熟雞蛋孵不出小雞。

——德國諺語

You can't hatch chickens from fried eggs.　　　—German proverb

962

細心的照顧要比漂亮的馬廄更能養出駿馬。

——丹麥諺語

Care, and not fine stables, makes a good horse.

—Danish proverb

963

時常被四處移植的樹木，難以繁茂。

——法蘭德斯諺語

Trees often transplanted seldom prosper.　　　—Flemish proverb

964

烤熟的鴿子不會平白無故飛進你的嘴巴。

—— 荷蘭諺語

Roasted pigeons will not fly into one's mouth.

—Dutch proverb

965

早起的鳥兒有蟲吃。

—— 英文諺語

The early bird catches the worm.

—English proverb

966

一個不願面對宿命的人，總會在逃避的路上遭遇他的宿命。

—— 法國諺語

One meets his destiny often in the road he takes to avoid it.

—French proverb

967
貓兒不在，鼠輩橫行。

—— 法國諺語

When the cat's away, the mice will play.

—French proverb

968
無論黑貓白貓，在黑暗中看起來都一樣是灰的。

—— 英文諺語

All cats appear grey in the dark.

—English proverb

969
好奇心殺死一隻貓。

—— 英文諺語

Curiosity killed the cat.

—English proverb

970

你不能同時在兩場婚禮上跳舞，就好像你不能
同時騎在兩匹馬的背上。

—— 意第緒諺語

You can't dance at two weddings at the same time; nor can you sit on
two horses with one behind. ——Yiddish proverb

971

當宮殿裡有鼠輩肆虐時，一隻瘸貓要比一匹駿
馬管用多了。

—— 世界諺語

When rats infest the palace, a lame cat is better than the swiftest horse.
——Proverb found in many cultures

972

貪睡的狗，就任牠繼續躺下去吧。

—— 法國諺語

Let sleeping dogs lie. ——French proverb

973

海裡有的是魚：依舊有合適的人在等著你。

—— 英文諺語

There are plenty more fish in the sea. —English proverb

974

那些跟你說別人閒話的人，也會跟別人說你的閒話。

—— 西班牙諺語

Whoever gossips to you will gossip about you.

—Spanish proverb

975

渡河時別更換坐騎。

—— 荷蘭諺語

Don't change horses in the middle of the stream.

—Dutch proverb

976

你可以將一匹馬牽到河邊，但你無法強迫牠喝水。

—— 英文諺語

You can lead a horse to water, but you can't make him drink.

—English proverb

977

在馬兒已脫韁而去之後才想到要關上馬廄的門，已經太遲了。

—— 法國諺語

It's too late to close the stable door after the horse has bolted.

—French proverb

978

即便是一生都在賣蠟燭的人，最後也將在黑暗中死去。

—— 哥倫比亞諺語

Even the candle seller dies in the dark.

—Colombian proverb

979
拜訪朋友的路途絕不遙遠。

——丹麥諺語

A road to a friend's house is never long.　　　　——Danish proverb

980
河童也會溺水；人都有失足的時候。

——日本諺語

Even professional swimmers can be drowned; anyone can make a mistake.　　　　——Japanese proverb

981
兩隻大象搏鬥，受傷最深的是草原。

——非洲諺語

When two elephants fight it is the grass that suffers.

——African proverb

982

無為者無誤。

—— 義大利諺語

He who does nothing makes no mistakes. —Italian proverb

983

在一扇門關上的同時，千百扇其他的門也為你開啟。

—— 西班牙諺語

When one door shuts, a hundred open. —Spanish proverb

984

貪得無厭之人的寶庫中唯一缺少的東西，就是友情。

—— 愛爾蘭諺語

The greedy man stores all but friendship. —Irish proverb

985

小錢不去，大錢不來。

—— 中國諺語

If a little money does not go out, great money will not come in.
—Chinese proverb

986

沒有歷史的民族，在這世上不會留下任何痕跡。

—— 拉科塔蘇族諺語

A people without history is like the wind on the buffalo grass.
—Lakota Sioux proverb

987

分享能使喜悅倍增，分擔能使悲傷減半。

—— 瑞典諺語

Joy shared is twice the joy. Sorrow shared is half the sorrow.
—Swedish proverb

988
若話說得不多，說錯了也容易補救。

—— 愛爾蘭諺語

Least said, soonest mended. —Irish proverb

989
富有人家的孩子，時常是由窮苦人家的母親看照著。

—— 丹麥諺語

A rich child often sits in a poor mother's lap. —Danish proverb

990
愚昧之人很快就會失去其財富。

—— 英文諺語

A fool and his money are soon parted. —English proverb

991

憂慮能夠讓一件小事產生巨大的陰影。

——瑞典諺語

Worry gives a small thing a big shadow. —Swedish proverb

992

天助自助者。

——伊索寓言〈大力士與馬伕〉

The gods help them that help themselves.
—*Aesop*, "Hercules and the Waggoner"

993

企圖模仿孔雀的麻雀，很有可能落得斷腿的下場。

——緬甸諺語

Sparrows that emulate peacocks are likely to break a thigh.
—Burmese proverb

994

在你沒有穿過他的鞋走上個兩個月之前,別輕易地評斷別人。

—— 美洲原住民諺語

Do not judge a man until you have walked two moons in his moccasins.
　　　　　　　　　—Native American proverb

995

無論夜晚多麼漫長,黎明終會到來。

—— 非洲諺語

However long the night, the dawn will break.
　　　　　　　　　—African proverb

996

事物的表象總是充滿欺騙性。

—— 伊索寓言〈野狼與羔羊〉

Appearances often are deceiving.
　　　　　　　　　—*Aesop*, "The Wolf and the Lamb"

997

貪口小心噎著了。

—— 義大利諺語

Big mouthfuls often choke.

—Italian proverb

998

親近生慢侮。

—— 伊索寓言〈狐狸與獅子〉

Familiarity breeds contempt.

—*Aesop*, "The Fox and the Lion"

999

賜子千金，不如賜子一技。

—— 中國諺語

Giving your son a skill is better than giving him one thousand pieces of gold.

—Chinese proverb

1000

如果你希望別人認為你是睿智的人，就同意他們的任何意見。

——意第緒諺語

If you want people to think you are wise, agree with them.

—Yiddish proverb

1001

那些能自我解嘲的人有福了，因為他們將永遠都感到快樂。

——世界諺語

Blessed is the man who can laugh at himself, for he will never cease to be amused.

—Proverb found in many cultures